5456

I0663333

Hill Daughter

Hill Daughter
New & Selected Poems

Louise McNeill

Edited and with an Introduction
by Maggie Anderson

University of Pittsburgh Press

Published by the University of Pittsburgh Press, Pittsburgh, Pa. 15260
Copyright © 1991, Louise McNeill
Introduction and Editor's Note copyright © 1991, Maggie Anderson
All rights reserved
Eurospan, London
Manufactured in the United States of America

LIBRARY OF CONGRESS CATALOGING-IN-PUBLICATION DATA

McNeill, Louise.
    Hill daughter : new and selected poems / Louise McNeill ; edited and with an
introduction by Maggie Anderson.
      p.   cm.
    Includes bibliographical references.
    ISBN 0-8229-3685-2.—ISBN 0-8229-5456-7 (pbk.)
     1. Mountain life—West Virginia—Poetry.   I. Anderson, Maggie.
II. Title.
PS3525.A283H55   1991
811'.52—dc20   91-8429
                                              CIP

Poems from *Elderberry Flood* are reprinted by permission of Elderberry
Books. Poems from *Time Is Our House* are reprinted by permission of
Middlebury College.

    Thirty-seven poems from *Paradox Hill* are published by permission
of the West Virginia University Press. Copyright 1972 by the West
Virginia University Foundation and the WVU Press on behalf of the
West Virginia University Libraries. All rights reserved.

To my husband, Roger Pease (1898–1990)

Rog and I were married for fifty-one years. His hand and sometimes his red pencil had touched the pages of several of the books from which the poems in *Hill Daughter* were selected. He knew, also, my old box of scraps. Some of these dusty lyrics had been lying in the box for fifty years. But in the midsummer of 1990 Maggie and I dug them out and picked representative poems to add to *Hill Daughter*. The poems in *Hill Daughter* cover sixty years of my writing (1931–1991).

L. McN.

If somewhere in the cooling rocks
Of cosmic seas, of cosmic dunes,
You find this thing of paradox
And can decipher out the runes
Upon these pages edged with scorch,
Forgive their tinges of the fire;
I flung them like a riven torch
Above the rupture of the pyre;
They billowed in a greenish blast;
And, with them, belling far away,
I heard the hound dogs of the past
Upon the burning mountains bay.

Paradox Hill

Contents

Contents

Contents

Contents

Introduction
Maggie Anderson

LOUISE NCNEILL was the first poet I heard give a poetry
reading. In 1964, I was sixteen years old and McNeill came to
read at the junior college in Keyser, West Virginia, where I
lived. I had read very little poetry and, except for the few
poems by Emily Dickinson in my school anthology, I had
read no poems by women. I knew nothing about the litera-
ture of my region and so, although I had decided by that time
that I wanted to be a poet, it would never have occurred to
me to write about my place, about West Virginia, or about
anything that I really knew and believed. When I first heard
Louise McNeill read her poems, I felt the strength of affirma-
tion for what I did not even know I had been denied.

Of that evening, I remember most clearly McNeill's stat-
ure. I thought she was, possibly, the tallest woman I had
ever seen, though perhaps the resonance of her voice made
her seem taller than she really was. I remember she wore
a blue dress, and a hat, and when she stood to read, she
walked out from behind the lectern and did not read, but
recited, the title poem of this collection, "Hill Daughter."
Her voice was strong and musical, and she had an unmistak-
able mountain accent, deep and nasal, twanging at the heart:

> Land of my fathers and blood, oh my fathers, whatever
> Is left of your grudge in the rock, of your hate in the stone;
> I have brought you at last what you sternly required that I
>   bring you,
> And have brought it alone.
>
> ("Hill Daughter," 1–4)

I knew nothing then of what I would later come to under-
stand of the requirements that patriarchy imposes on women,
or of what it means to be a woman who must offer her son
up to that system. But, as a young girl from the Appala-
chian Mountains, I understood quite a lot about rocks and

stones and grudges, and any young girl anywhere would have then (or now) understood about fathers and their stern requirements.

I can still remember most of the poems McNeill read that evening: some of the character poems from *Gauley Mountain;* a few of her "Overheard on a Bus" poems that made poetry of the ordinary mountain speech I had heard all my life; and "How to Unbewitch a Backtracking Hound." It would be many years before I would come to understand the complexity and subtlety that lie beneath even McNeill's apparently simple poems: the poised promise in "First Flight," for example, that presumes other occasions when the speaker "lifted [her] arms up and flapped them and flew." Louise McNeill understands the sources of poetry in memory, in the wordplay of chant and rhyme, and in the joy of mouthing musical sounds. I heard the beat of her unique music in the poems that night and responded to it deeply. Through more than twenty years of reading Louise McNeill's poems, I have learned also to hear the complexity embedded in them, and I admire her work greatly still for both of these things.

Louise McNeill was born in 1911 in Pocahontas County, West Virginia, on a farm that her family had lived on for nine generations. In the foreword to her first full-length volume of poems, *Gauley Mountain,* published in 1939, Stephen Vincent Benet wrote: "She has come to her work through birthright, not through a self-conscious attempt to follow a fashion in Americana and the work shows it. . . . [These] are West Virginians and this is a West Virginia book."[1]

---

1. *Gauley Mountain* (New York: Harcourt Brace, 1939; rpt. Parsons, W. V.: McClain Printing Company, 1960, 1990), p. xii. Kaleidoscope Press in Dallas, Texas, published a limited edition chapbook of Louise McNeill's poems, *Mountain White,* in 1931, but *Gauley Mountain* was her first full-length volume.

Introduction

Throughout the 1930s American writers were finding out who they were as Americans by articulating themselves as midwesterners, southerners, New Englanders, Californians, Jews, or African-Americans. They were in search of what Archibald MacLeish, Carl Sandburg, and others called "The People." A short list of some of these writers shows that "The People" had turned out to be wonderfully diverse: Edgar Lee Masters, Sinclair Lewis, Sherwood Anderson, and Meridel LeSueur from the Midwest; John Steinbeck, Mary Hunter Austin and Robinson Jeffers from the West; Robert Frost and Edwin Arlington Robinson from New England; Claude McKay, Langston Hughes, Nella Larsen, and Zora Neale Hurston from the Harlem of the Harlem Renaissance; Henry Roth, Anzia Yezierska, Tess Slesinger and Muriel Rukeyser from New York City; and James Agee, Thomas Wolfe, Jesse Stuart, and Elizabeth Madox Roberts from the South and from the Appalachian Mountains. Titles are also indicative of the preoccupations of the regional, populist literature of this period: Langston Hughes, *Ways of White Folks* (1934); Tess Slesinger, *The Unpossessed* (1934); Sherwood Anderson, *Puzzled America* (1935); Edgar Lee Masters, *Poems of People* (1936); Carl Sandburg, *The People, Yes* (1936); Claude McKay, *A Long Way from Home* (1937); Sinclair Lewis, *My America* (1938); Muriel Rukeyser, *U.S. 1* (1938); and Thomas Wolfe, *You Can't Go Home Again* (1940).

When Stephen Vincent Benet hailed Louise McNeill as "a new poet in the land," she entered a literary climate hospitable to diversity, including writings by and about rural, small town, poor, and poorly educated men and women.[2] Benet was correct in his assertion that what Louise McNeill was doing was not simply an "attempt to follow a fashion."

2. Ibid., p. xi.

Introduction

In her memoirs, *The Milkweed Ladies,* Louise McNeill introduces herself:

> Until I was sixteen years old, until the roads came, the farm was about all I knew: our green meadows and hilly pastures, our storied old men, the great rolling seasons of moon and sunlight, our limestone cliffs and trickling springs. It was about all I knew, and, except for my father and before him, the old Rebel Captain, all that any of us had ever known: just the farm and our little village down at the crossroads, and the worn cowpaths winding the slopes; or we kids driving the cows home in the summer evenings; or the winter whiteness and stillness, Aunt Malindy's "old woman in the sky" picking her geese, and the "old blue misties" sweeping out of the north.[3]

When a people sets out to define itself, one of the first tasks is historical documentation. Louise McNeill published a small chapbook of lyric poems, *Mountain White,* in 1931 when she was twenty years old, but it is not surprising that her first full-length collection, *Gauley Mountain* (1939), was a verse history. These poems narrate the settling of a fictional land called "Gauley" by the first white people who crossed the Allegheny Mountains into western Virginia. They follow the imagined lives of these people from the 1700s to the coming of the roads and the timber industry. The poetic strategies in *Gauley Mountain* are similar to those in Edgar Lee Masters's *Spoon River Anthology* (1915), a work to which McNeill's has often been compared, but she writes with more affection for the people and attempts a larger historical and political scope.

In the years between the two world wars, during and just after the Great Depression, American writers were in search

---

3. Louise McNeill, *The Milkweed Ladies* (Pittsburgh, Pa.: University of Pittsburgh Press, 1988), p. 5.

of their "People," assessing their particular strengths and resources. Readers and critics of the 1930s valued the writings of people from the southern Appalachian Mountains for their historical consciousness, their connection to the land and the governing rhythms of the seasons, and for their fierce pride and willingness to defend both kin and country. Reviews of Louise McNeill's *Gauley Mountain* praised its "straightforwardness" and its "vigor" and found "a poetical intonation deep within it and a strength and ruggedness which must emanate from Gauley Mountain itself and from [McNeill's] ancestors who settled there."[4]

Louise McNeill's journey out of West Virginia into what is sometimes called in the mountains "the outside world" started in 1938 when she won the Atlantic Monthly Poetry Prize, began publishing regularly in that magazine, and traveled "over the mountain"[5] to New England where she studied at the Bread Loaf Writers' Conference with Robert Frost and met Roger Pease, who would become her "hardheaded, earth-loving Yankee school-master husband."[6] In the fall of 1938, McNeill had a fellowship to the University of Iowa Writers' Workshop where she was a first reader with Jean Stafford for the magazine *American Prefaces*.[7] McNeill met Archibald MacLeish in the spring of 1939, and he took the manuscript of what would become *Gauley Mountain* to New York. Louise McNeill and Roger Pease were married

---

4. *Book of the Month Club Review,* August 1939; *The Globe* (Boston), October 21, 1939.

5. McNeill, *The Milkweed Ladies,* p. 113.

6. Ibid., p. 114.

7. *American Prefaces,* "a journal of critical and imaginative writing," was published from 1935 to 1943 under the auspices of the School of Letters and with the cooperation of the School of Journalism and the School of Fine Arts at the University of Iowa.

in the summer of 1939, shortly before the publication of *Gauley Mountain,* and they began what McNeill has called their "wandering through all the years of the Second World War."[8]

In 1942, Middlebury College Press in Vermont published the last of a series of chapbooks printed by the Bread Loaf printers, a volume of poems by Louise McNeill called *Time Is Our House.* McNeill and her husband had had a son, their only child, and were teaching at a boys' preparatory school in South Carolina. Although McNeill continued to publish poems and some fiction and articles in magazines fairly regularly in the years that followed, her next volume of poems, *Paradox Hill: From Appalachia to Lunar Shore,* was not published until 1972.

Both the literary climate and the lives of most Americans had changed dramatically in those intervening thirty years. By the 1950s, the literary populism, inclusiveness, and diversity of the 1930s had given way to the intellectual agenda of the New Criticism. The countercultural movements of the fifties (the Beats, the Black Mountain writers, and the New York poets) were predominantly white, male, and urban. Most of the few women poets who began publishing in the 1950s, radical as they often were in their understandings of both feminism and its broader political contexts, led lives considerably more privileged than Louise McNeill's. Poetic and fictional documentation of the lives of rural and working-class people was kept alive through these years by small regional presses, but by the late fifties, "regional" had become a pejorative adjective when applied to a work of literature. "The People" had gone back to wherever they had briefly arisen from, and it had come to seem that these

---

8. McNeill, *The Milkweed Ladies,* p. 114. Louise McNeill and Roger Pease were married for fifty-one years. Roger Pease died in the fall of 1990.

lives were no longer of any particular interest except to those who lived them. The populist literature of the 1930s had been relegated to historical eccentricity, and was, until very recently, effectively erased from the literary canon.

The work of many writers from the southern Appalachian Mountains is a record of painful journeyings, away from what Kentucky poet James Still has called "the earth loved more than any other earth," off to the bright promise and the brighter economies of the cities.9 Louise McNeill's life and work reflect these journeyings. The "paradox," as she has named it, is, in part, that the very opportunities that call mountain writers away from home also cut them off from the deepest sources of the writing itself, from its original impulses in a beloved place and people. McNeill's 1972 book, *Paradox Hill,* containing over one hundred poems in a fully developed and wide-ranging voice, records these separations. The poems reflect her attempt to find some balance between the world she had grown up in (a world which, to a large extent, no longer existed) and the world she had traveled to and learned from "over the mountain." In addition, the poems in *Paradox Hill* document the dizzying rate of change in the sixty years since the coming of the roads, the timber and mining industries, the chemical plants and the glass factories, and their effects on the culture of the mountain people. In 1959, Louise McNeill received a doctorate in history from West Virginia University, and she taught English and history in West Virginia colleges and universities for nearly twenty years. The poems in *Paradox Hill* are written in the authentic voice of an insider to the culture, one who

9. James Still, "Wolfpen Creek," *The Wolfpen Poems* (Berea, Ky.: Berea College Press, 1968), p. 71.

is also a trained historian and an accomplished poet who had read widely and traveled far.

The North Carolina writer, Fred Chappell, has noted that "the Appalachian poet (if he is not a songwriter or a folk poet) will write in a double idiom, both in the language indigenous to his region and in the accepted language of literary discourse which he learned at school or from books."[10] Louise McNeill's rhythms and her concerns mark her, unmistakably, as a writer of the southern mountain culture. She uses the ballad form deftly, adapts the structures of the mountain tall tale to her verse, and rhythmically employs what Stephen Vincent Benet had recognized as "the high, shrill notes of the mountain fiddle."[11] Although linguistic dis-ease is only one of several homesicknesses an Appalachian will experience when he or she leaves the mountains, one of the most complex tasks for any writer from this region is to employ this "double idiom" artfully. In *Paradox Hill* especially, McNeill's poems stay close to the common speech of home while, at the same time, interweaving her considerable knowledge of history, science, and metrical verse. In "Poet," for example, she presents a rather complex, metaphysical view of what a poet is and does, aesthetically sophisticated and eloquent: "I am trajectory and flight" and "the swift parabola of light" (1, 3); yet the poem concludes on a musically phrased line directly out of the West Virginia mountains in both image and diction:

> The falling feather of the cock,
> The point, propulsion, and the flood
> Of blackbirds twanging from the nock
> And I the target and the blood.
> ("Poet," 5–8)

10. Fred Chappell, "Double Language: Three Appalachian Poets," *Appalachian Journal* 8 (Autumn 1980): 55.
11. Foreword to *Gauley Mountain*, p. xi.

In "Threnody for Old Orchards," McNeill metaphorcially puts on the "hairy garments" of Greek tragedy to lament in deep oracular tones the loss of the old orchards on the abandoned farms of her home country:

> Gone is that time and gone my orchard country,
> And all the fields and farmsteads of this plain;
> And all so lost—so lost—the hardhack tangles,
> And nettles choke the footpath and the lane—
>
> And all so lost—and all so lost forever—
> That had I, of the Greek, some tragic song,
> Here, from the sounding well of this old orchard,
> I would inflict my wrong
> On all the world, and all the world would answer,
> And draped in hairy garments, walk the stage,
> And cry the death of kinsmen and of orchards,
> And rage and rage and rage.
>   ("Threnody for Old Orchards," 9–20)

The "double idiom" is used by all poets to some extent, but it is particularly hard won for Appalachian writers, whose beautifully metaphorical and ungrammatical native speech has been stereotyped as ignorant. Writers from this region are often tempted to deny the language of home. Louise McNeill does not, and her best poems are written in a blended language that is colloquial, emotionally complex, and intellectually exacting.

In 1979, after her retirement from teaching, McNeill was appointed Poet Laureate of West Virginia. She was commissioned by the West Virginia Department of Culture and History to write a verse history of West Virginia for use by students in West Virginia public schools. This volume,

Elderberry Flood: The History, Lore and Land of West Virginia Written in Verse Form, is McNeill's most public and thus, her most political book. Unlike *Gauley Mountain,* which worked from anecdote and fictional characterization following a loose historical outline, *Elderberry Flood* uses historical accounts of West Virginia's past as the starting point for the poems. These are not, however, poems lacking in point of view. The best ones document the industrialization of the region: the coming of the roads and the first trains, the timber booms and the coal camps, the myriad "horsemen" who have traveled through West Virginia: "Buying the River Coal;" "Buying the Sandy, / Giving our little kids red sugar-candy" ("The Horsemen," 16, 19–20). The ironic poetic voice asks:

> Who are these horsemen here riding and roaming over our
>   forest trails?
> Why are they combing each little patch of pine here on the
>   river?
> See how the hemlocks shake—
> Why do they quiver?
>
> ("The Horsemen," 1–4)

Louis Untermeyer wrote that Louise McNeill's "ballad-like music . . . ranges from the matter-of-fact to the macabre."[12] In McNeill's work, the macabre is nowhere more evident than in the group of poems in *Paradox Hill* that concern the threat of nuclear holocaust. This group of poems begins with "Cassandra," in which the solitary woman seer (there are many solitary women in McNeill's poems) has recognized "the shape of a gaunt mushroom" and weaves "in [her] cloth that the world would die" (2, 4). In a

---

12. Louis Untermeyer, jacket comment for *Paradox Hill: From Appalachia to Lunar Shore* (Morgantown: West Virginia University Libraries, 1972).

moving and frightening retelling of an ancient Celtic tale
of two crows squabbling over one piece of meat, McNeill
presents "The New Corbies" who, after the nuclear holo-
caust, sit in a tree and argue over the burnt flesh of human
beings:

> The crows will find below them there,
> All blooming from the ground,
> As flowered and as fat a feast
> As crows have ever found.
>
> Of scarlet red and bloated white,
> And flowered full in bloom
> These tropic blossoms all will burst
> To waft their sweet perfume.
>   ("The New Corbies," 5–12)

In "Of Fitness to Survive," because the firefly and the
glowworm "By their burning are in tune / With the
structure of the atom"; they are the only ones rendered "im-
mune" (2–3, 4). They feast, creeping down "embered halls,"
"Sucking of the fire-milk flowing— / Lava from the fire-
hag's breast" (8, 11–12). McNeill's atomic poems are vivid,
even grisly, and her willingness to imagine the particulars of
the horror of nuclear holocaust is testament to her poetic
courage, as well as to how deeply she has loved the earth to
be able to grieve its possible extinction so fiercely.

In McNeill's poems on nuclear power and on the ques-
tionable benefits of space exploration ("The Runaway Team,"
"Lost in Orbit"), she shows a very contemporary under-
standing of the similar epistemologies of science and poetry.
In the last chapter of *The Milkweed Ladies,* "Night at the
Commodore," she recounts her first awareness of the in-
comprehensible power of the atomic bomb dropped on Hiro-
shima on August 4, 1945. McNeill understands what the

contemporary ecology movement is only now beginning to realize, and what very few of our poets have even begun to consider: that the possibility of the extinction of the planet means that we can never again view the natural world, or write about it, in the same confident, self-assured way the Romantic poets did.[13] Starkly, and with no trace of sentimentality, McNeill states the simple facts:

> That was the night the world changed. It wasn't joy that died, or faith, or resolution, for all these come back. It was something else, something deep and earth-given that died that night in the Commodore. Never again would I be able to say with such infinite certainty that the earth would always green in the springtime, and the purple hepaticas come to bloom on my woodland rock.[14]

I love the mountain songs and ballads of Louise McNeill, and I admire her considerable skill with anecdote and characterization. Her women characters, especially, appeal to me. They are almost always risk-takers, brazen and unorthodox, willing to bear the censure of the community, somewhat eccentric, "stiff-necked" and "impenitent" even on their deathbeds.[15] Very few women poets have written as straightforwardly and as honestly of the complex knot of the urge for life and the fear of death that accompany pregnancy and giving birth. In "Lullaby," McNeill gives this "paradox" a

13. One poet I think of in this context is also from the Appalachian region. James Wright wrote clearly enough of this necessary understanding in "Redwings": "It turns out / You can kill them. / It turns out / You can make the earth absolutely clean." *The Collected Poems of James Wright* (New York: Farrar Straus & Giroux, 1990), p. 283.

14. McNeill, *The Milkweed Ladies*, p. 122.

15. McNeill, "Jane Renick MacElmain," *Gauley Mountain*, p. 29. Cf. "Tillie Sage," ibid., p. 83.

distinctly political context when she asks her "sisters," other mothers, who "wear against [their] skin like some old garment / The unwashed thought of death" (7–8), to sing this "lullaby" to their children who are about to enter the world:

> *My child, unborn in darkness sleep,*
> *Take freely of my bone,*
> *And of my blood take all you need,*
> *Till you can walk alone.*
> *So live and grow and issue forth,*
> *And come prepared for war,*
> *Though sure, your mother does not know*
> *Which one she bears you for.*
> ("Lullaby," 12–20)

Louise McNeill is not a poet without hope for the future. She sees hope, particularly, in our intelligent connection to history and in our stewardship of what land there is left to tend. But she would find it foolish and sentimental to pretend that we live in a world that welcomes children more than war, or that is capable of eternal rejuvenation when we have much evidence (such as the fifteen million acres of West Virginia forest lost to the timber industry) that some things cannot come back. McNeill refuses to look away from the fact that we have developed a technology that can destroy all of the world, and all of us.

Louise McNeill is one of my essential poets. Quite simply, her poems have made my own poems possible. This volume brings back into print poems which have been unavailable for more than twenty years. For those of us from the Appalachian Mountains, this is cause for celebration. Those coming to Louise McNeill's work for the first time can look forward to musical, serious, idiosyncratic, and startling poems that will leave their view of the world irrevocably altered, and larger, for what she has to tell us from her own "place called solid," from her own "slow, archean peculiar stance."16

16. McNeill, *The Milkweed Ladies*, p. 8.

Editor's Note

THE POEMS in this collection are not arranged in chrono-
logical order of publication. Louise McNeill's poetic voice
has remained relatively consistent through a long writing life
while her concerns have deepened and changed. Some of her
books have been organized around a single theme or written
to an outline of historical events. She has often published
several poems on the same subject in different books. In
this collection, I have, with Louise McNeill's permission,
arranged the poems in groups that reflect the major con-
cerns of her poems, regardless of when they were written.
When poems from a single volume could be neatly grouped
together, I have done this: the character poems from *Gauley
Mountain* are included here in the section called "Gauley
Mountain"; poems on the coming of the roads and the in-
dustries to West Virginia from *Elderberry Flood* are grouped
in the section called "The Horsemen." In other cases, early
poems have been grouped with later, or new and unpublished
poems, because they have a similar subject matter or tone.
In all cases, I have worked toward an ordering that would
be clear, accessible, and reflective of McNeill's several consis-
tent concerns. A list of all of Louise McNeill's published
volumes with the poems taken from each is included at the
end of this book.

I am grateful to Peter Oresick at the University of Pitts-
burgh Press for his consistent support of this project and for
his assistance with the final manuscript. I am also grateful to
Irene McKinney and Devon McNamara, who share my en-
thusiasm for the poems of Louise McNeill and whose think-
ing about them has helped shape my own. The Research
Council of Kent State University provided me with a re-
search leave in the fall of 1990 which helped me to complete
this work, and I appreciate their support, as well as that of
the MacDowell Colony, where much of the work was done.

Editor's Note

I am also grateful to Jane Cooper, Anne Hobson Freeman, Hilary Sio, and Jacqueline Woodson for their support and intelligent responses to the introduction. I am deeply grateful to Louise McNeill, who gave her permission for me to edit this collection, who informed all of my thinking about it.

M.A.

Hill Daughter

Memoria

I have never heard them;
I shall never hear—
Still an echo falling
When the night is clear,
In the darkness wakes me
Like a trumpet's call:
Wild swans crying
Southward in the fall.

Warning

Walk through the fern but do not tear the root.
Rest on the stump but count no ring of age.
In rotting wood see neither hint nor sign,
Nor translate from the oak leaf's fallen page
One mystic line.

Look at the wheat field, see it blade and straw,
But neither bread nor sealed-in germ nor shadowy reaper—
Leave the close ground its anonymity,
Such knowledge to the blind mole and the worm—
The gray night-creeper.

Leave the enigma to the close-lipped dark;
Beyond your fenced-in land do not inquire—
For things there be best hidden:
Light that only the blind should see—
And over the hills in that far country
Truth bare, forbidden.

Blizzard

In the blizzard night,
Bringing the cattle down from the hills,
We heard in our capped ears
The soundless screaming,
Sniffed in the ripped air the scent that has no smell,
Felt with our gloved fingers
The stiff bone formless and white,
Saw with our whipped eyes the shape unshadowed—

Only our blood recalled,
And the cattle calling
Answered the fear up there on the primal hilltops,
Where the frost grass whined,
And the naked thing crouched waiting.

Snow Angels

Martin, Stevie, and Joe, and I,
Four in our family, long ago,
One winter day on the road to school,
Boot-top high through a field of snow,
Stopped by the old black walnut tree;
And Joe and Martin and I, all three,
Lay on our backs in a laughing row,
Our white forms printed. The tall one Joe;
Mart beside him; the fat one, me.
Then we called to Stevie, "Look yonder, see,
Angels resting beneath the tree!"

But Steve had paused by the open spring,
Down on his knees in the yellow mud,
Watching his face in the troubled pool
Where the snow birds drank and the cattle trod—
"Look, Steve, angels." But he just stepped
His muddy tracks where the angels slept.

Mart and Stevie and Joe and I,
Four in our family, long ago.
Then three white winds past the walnut tree—
Joe and Martin and I, all three—

For pollen scatters; the leaf must blow;
The winged seed follow the squall of snow—
The winged seed follow, the field lie clear—

  (Mart in China, a card last year—
  Joe in Houston, a yacht and plane—
  And here by the mirror I lift my hands,
  Binding my throat with a velvet chain—
  The skin of my throat and the sharpening bone.)

Wind past the tree and the snow-whirls blown—
In the hands of our angels the wheat seed sown;
Over their bodies the wheat stalks mown.

But Stevie's tracks from the meadow spring
Still break the stubble and print the clay,
And his steps zigzag with the cradle's swing,
So near the place where our angels lay.

One earth-born shape with his shoulders low—
Four in our family, long ago.

American Boating Song

(1939)

Drift, drift, do not lift
Your birch pole from the river.
Let the arrow grasses grow
In their reedy quiver.
Let the arrow grasses grow
In their moveless shallow
Underneath the moon-strung bow
Of a leaning willow.

Drift, drift, do not turn
Near that clump of arrows.
On each side the fox fires burn
Warning of the narrows.
Drift, drift, do not pause
Where those arrows sway.
Who would see them bring to earth
The dead white bird of day?

Mayapple Hill

Children warned against the Mandrake—
Apple of the twisted root,
On the hilltop every summer,
Suckle at the golden fruit;
Suck the pale exotic fragrance,
Revel in the mellow pome—
Children, drunken with the sunlight,
In the evening stagger home—
Nor at bedtime sense the fever,
Nor at morning any chill—
Taken from the tumored apple,
Golden on the August hill.

All the children of the summer
Sleeping drowsy in the sun
Of the upland, August meadow—
With their golden fevers done—
Children of the earth who reveled
In the sweetness of the fruit—
Lying with their limbs disheveled
In the Mandrake's twisted root—
Children of the twisted torsos,
Lying always, oh, so still—
Where the Mandrake's tumored apples
Ripen mellow on the hill.

Poet

I am trajectory and flight—
The archer, arrow, and the bow—
The swift parabola of light—
And I the rising and the flow,
The falling feather of the cock,
The point, propulsion, and the flood
Of blackbirds twanging from the nock,
And I the target and the blood.

The Dream

I tried to move,
    But I could make no motion;
I tried to scream,
    But all my screams were gone;
I tried to see,
    But fog was lapped around me—
I lay upon my face, yet saw my spine,
And every bone there seemed to shine—
My country's bones?
    Or were they mine?

Each vertebra a coin of gold
Set deeply in my flesh and skin—
Set deeply there and hammered in
Until because of gold—its love—
I could not move—
    I tried to move—

Lullaby

Herda, herda, herda, sing my sisters
Who retch in the early morning and at noon,
Who wake in the night and walk splayfooted, careful,
Nine months beneath the moon;
All who are swaybacked and with wombs protruding,
Swollen and short of breath,
And wear against your skin like some old garment
The unwashed thought of death.
Sit with me now, and in the cool of evening,
Rock what you carry in your hammocked caul,
And sing this lullaby while on the wall,
The pale leaves tremble, sing:

My child, unborn in darkness sleep,
Take freely of my bone,
And of my blood take all you need,
Till you can walk alone.
So live and grow and issue forth,
And come prepared for war,
Though sure, your mother does not know
Which one she bears you for.

Aubade to Fear
(Heavy with Child)

Last night as I lay cold with fear
Of my travail now drawing near,
A gray wind I no longer hear
Blew from the darkness over me—
Blew southward from the Norn-white skies
Until I slept with seeing eyes—
Seeing no bauble fit to prize.

Not seeing dawn, its thin gray trace
Turn gold upon the pillow lace
And touch the warm beloved face.
Not seeing all I lived to own:
The torque of rubies, stone by stone,
The living pages touched and known.

Seeing instead that nets are small
Which shield us from the sparrow's fall,
How frail the rooftree and the wall,
How thin the string by which we tie
Our great ships of the wind and sky—
And what a little thing to die.

Second Sight
(My Son's First Springtime)

Since to look at earth through his eyes
Is light to see
The greener leaf on the greater tree
And the petals blown by a wondrous breath,
I have this urgency for death.

For once myself I stood alone
And watched the white bloom whiter blown—
The leaves grew outward from the bough
As green as I remember now,
When through him I again regard
Spring re-created and unmarred.

Dear God, I could not now behold
The wonder fading and grown old,
Nor do I care to see through him
The gray cross thrusting from the limb.

Hill Daughter

Land of my fathers and blood, oh my fathers, whatever
Is left of your grudge in the rock, of your hate in the stone;
I have brought you at last what you sternly required that I
    bring you,
And have brought it alone.

I, who from the womb must be drawn, though the first born,
    a daughter,
And could never stand straight with the rifle, nor lean with
    the plow;
Here is ease for the curse, here is cause for the breaking of
    silence.
You can answer me now.

It has taken me long to return, and you died without
    knowing,
But down where the veins of the rock and the aspen tree
    run—
Land of my fathers and blood, oh my fathers, whatever
Is left of your hearts in the dust,
I have brought you a son.

🌳 *Wire Brier*

I call no muse, for the sandaled foot
Should never tread where the brogan lumbers.
I have gulled the pith from a sumac limb
To play a tune that my blood remembers.

Gauley Mountain

Fox and Geese

Let us make a circle here—
Round and round we go
Till our feet have made this ring
Beaten in the snow.

Let us cross it now with paths—
Crisscross passing by,
Back and forth, until our trails
Cut it like a pie.

Let us play at Fox and Geese,
Run and chase and sing,
Play the world is still at peace,
And our world a ring
Made by children in the snow of this meadow long ago,
Children of the sun and snow—
Children of the sun.

Hill Song

The ferns are in the fiddlehead, fiddlehead;
The ferns are in the fiddlehead.
The service tree in the woods is white;
The wild crab sheds its fragrant light;
The bullfrogs boom from the crick at night—
And the ferns are in the fiddlehead.

Faldang

Cider in the rain barrel, corn in the popper,
Shoats in the mast woods, mash in the hopper,
Taffy on the windowsill, rosin on the bow,
Grab your partners, Boys, dance the "Do Si Do"!

Logs in the fireplace, pone in the baker,
Taters in their jacket coats, salt in the shaker,
Kick the rhythm with your heel, catch it on your toe,
Grab your partners, Boys, dance the "Hoe Down Hoe"!

Pick and shovel in the loft, boss man under kivver,
Dishpan in the chicken yard, boat gone down the river,
Rags stuffed in the broken pane, wind a-howlin' low,
Grab your partners, Boys, "How you oughta know"!

"Old Dan Tucker," "Old Zip Coon,"
"Old Ninety-Seven," any old tune!
Pat-a-foot, Granny! Break down, Ma!
Hug-em-tight, Annie! Step high, Pa!

Cider in the rain barrel, corn in the popper,
Shoats in the mast woods, mash in the hopper,
Taffy on the windowsill, rosin on the bow,
Grab your partners, dance the "Do Si Do"!

Fiddler
(1976)

He took his mountain fiddle up
And sawed across the strings;
A birdsong strained its torrent out
Through green and silver rings;
And crickets came and picked it up
From hollows in the grass,
And then the fiddler played a train
That hooted through the pass—
Then changed his tune. A wildness came,
The chords of night were torn,
And lightning split its briery flame—
A burning tree of thorn
Lashed out and crashed across the hills;
And then the fiddler drew a quiet thread
And held it still . . .
Then cut the thread in two.
And there was laughter from the west;
A traveler wind arose;
The fiddler smiled and dipped his chin,
Began to tap his toes;
And "Turkey in the Straw" rang out!
The jig-time music beat;
And so we danced and danced and danced,
And whirled and stomped our feet,
And circled four and butterflied
And did the pigeon wing,
And sashayed round and bowed and scraped,
And had our golden fling—
Then out-of-breath . . .
The fiddler stopped.

He opened up his case
And put his birdsong in
And snapped the cover down in place—
His hooting train, his turkey call,
His thorny lightning tree—
And snapped the cover on them all
And locked it with his key.

Mountain Corn Song

Oak leaves are big as a gray squirrel's ear
And the dogwood bloom is white,
While down in the crick the bullfrogs boom
For a "Jug o' Rum" all night.
Out in the fields while the dawn is still
Four bright grains to each sandy hill
With, *"One for the beetle and one for the bee
One for the devil and one for me."*

A drouth wind gasps and the clouds move on
So the red clay fields bake dry,
But pea vines throttle the green young blades,
And the grass stands boot-top high.
This is the time for scraping the hoe
Around each plant in the hard-packed row,
*"One stalk for the smut and one for the weed,
One for the borer and one for need."*

A drizzle sinks in the stubble field
And the wigwam shocks are brown,
While under the thorny, brush-pile fence
The leaves are bedded down,
So this is the season to kneel in muck
And strip each ear from its withered shuck,
With, *"One for dodger and one to feed,
One for likker and one for seed."*

Moonshiner

In a cave at the mouth of Dead Man's Holler
Where the wild plums claw and the black haws twine
To cover the entrance, thorn and bramble,
I tend my kittles and still my shine.
Grain a-work in my barrels and noggins,
Corn and barley and rye and wheat.
A quart of ashes to make it sour. . . .
A poke of sugar to keep it sweet. . . .
A can of lye so the stuff will fizzle,
Fizzle, sizzle, and foam and swell. . . .
Limestone water to make it clearer
Than rain on a huckleberry bell.

In a cave at the mouth of Dead Man's Holler
Where the hills are close and the rocks are steep,
With my kittles red and the brass worm dripping
I work while the Revenooers sleep.
Bile and bubble and steam and trickle. . . .
Jugs and bottles and jars to fill.
In a cave at the mouth of Dead Man's Holler,
With my skunk gun handy, I run my still.

Wire Brier

Let us remember, here recall
Old rhymes chanted when we were small:
Never, never to step on cracks;
Beware of hoptoads with warty backs;
And, "A bushel of wheat—a bushel of rye;
Who's not ready holler I."

Let us remember, live again
Twilight evenings when we were ten,
With hide-and-seek on the summer lawn,
The fireflies lighting us off and on;
And how we ran to the old yard tree
And touched it, shouting our one, two, three—
"A bushel of wheat and a bushel of clover;
Who's not ready can't hide over."

Involved
(The Spider)

Lying on the hilltop
In the grasses tall,
Forest of the grasses
And myself so small,
Underneath the grass trees
In the sunny shine,
I saw the biggest spider
With eyes as big as mine;
And they were growing larger still,
For in them I could see
A little, tiny brown girl
Who looked like me;
And in her little brown eyes
I saw a spider crawl,
And in that little spider's eyes
A girl so very small
I just could see her eyes glint,
And in the glint there shone
A little, wee spider
Staring all alone. . . .
He stared at me so softly
I jumped up to run
And stepped on a spider mite;
Then blood was in the sun—
A little spot of mite blood
On the grasses' shine,
And in that blood a little drop
Of blood as red as mine.

Overheard on a Bus
(Woman with a Cleft Palate)

My husband up and left—gone away.
But me, I'm keeping on. I work by day.
It's my old Dad-in-law. He's not my own,
But still I call him "Pa"—
Eighty-five and down in bed—
Sort of touchy. It's his head.
But Pa—well, he—
Always say he treated me
Good enough. It's turn about—
It's hard, they tell me;
Say, to put him out.
But I ain't got no people of my own.

Chestnut Orchard

Saturday morning—no school today,
And we are up in the smoky dawn,
Hunting our sugar pokes from the press,
Putting our heavy stockings on.

Up the path to the chestnut grove,
Over the fence—first you, then I.
Acres of leaves for our scuffling feet,
And the rich burrs open against the sky.

A stick for you and a stick for me—
Sticks to scatter the leaves that hide—
Then the shining nuts with their silver tails,
And we bend and pick from the brown hillside.

Plenty for you and plenty for me,
And a bushel left for the gray squirrel's store,
And all the morning the squirrels and we,
In our golden house with its leafy floor.

Saturday morning—no school today.
This last gold harvest before the snow—
Let us go up to the chestnut trees.
It is Saturday morning and we must go,

Back through the years beyond time and space,
On a hill—by a dream—we will find that place,
And the great trees standing, untouched by blight,
In the silver fog and the golden light.

Once when I was little and played on the hill,
One wondrous evening, I dream of it still—
Mom called me to dinner, impatient, I knew—
So I lifted my arms up and flapped them and flew.

I lifted my arms up and flapped them, and lo!
I was flying as fast as my short legs could go.
The hill swirled beneath me, all foggy and green;
I lit by the yard fence, and no one had seen.

I told them at dinner, I said, "I can fly."
They laughed, not believing. I started to cry
And ran from the table, and sobbed, "It is true—
You need not believe me; I flapped and I flew."

I told them next morning; I told them again—
For years I kept telling; they laughed and I ran—
No one would believe me; I ceased then to tell;
But still I remember, remember it well—

One soft summer evening up there on the knoll,
Before life had harried the reach of my soul,
I stood there in twilight, in childlight, and dew—
And I lifted my arms up and flapped them and flew!

Lost in Orbit

Lost in orbit and passed Earth by—
And on forever—around and round—
Over the tracks that the comets fly—
Searched forever but never found—
And never grow older and never die,
And never a grave on the hilly ground.

How to Unbewitch a Backtracking Hound

If your hound dog runs the backtrack,
You can make him switch—
Just you foller what I tell you,
Likely there's a witch somewhere;
Just write out the Lord's Prayer,
Write it on a scroll
Made of bearskin—when you've writ it,
Roll it careful in a roll,
Bake it in a batch of cornbread—
When it's baked and brown,
Take it hot out to the dog trot,
Feed it to your hound.

Ballad of Joe Bittner

Joe Bittner, he was a mountain lad,
And he went to the second war—
Joined the navy for good or bad
And sailed where the bloodbills are—

Solomon Islands—the place he died
When his burning ship sucked deep—
And the letter came, and his mother cried,
And he slept where the war whales sleep.

We held his wake at his mother's house—
In the churchyard held his prayer—
And we wrote his name on the golden board
That sits in our courthouse square.

It was fourteen years, on a summer day,
When I looked at my yard fence stile,
And I saw the ghost of a sailor's sway
And Joe Bittner's cocky smile.

"Joe Bittner! Joe Bittner! Where have you been?
When your ship went down that night—
And we thought—we heard"—Then he grinned at me:
"Well—I never was much to write."

Stories at Evening
(A Suburban Mother Tells Stories to Her Son)

My great great grandpa Jethro walked
The wild savannahs deep in grass;
He saw the herds of buffalo
File westward through the mountain pass.

Great grandpa William in his time
Remembered pigeons wild and gray
Whose thousand wings beat out the sun
The morning that they flew away.

My grandpa Frederick could recall
The wild trout flashing in their school;
He set his stick of dynamite
And scooped a hundred from the pool.

My father, Douglas, saw the trees.
Across this bare, eroded land,
He saw the tulip tree and ash,
The spruce and hemlock—virgin stand.

And I myself at morning saw
The chestnut on the ridge—its living green—
The blue-fringed gentian . . .

Listen now, my son—
Stories at evening—wonders I have seen;
And as we sit, look sharp and well remember—
Your son may hear the strangest tale of all:
How little rabbits hopped across our garden,
How *grass* grew by the wall,
And there, one night, when you were six or seven,
You heard a bobwhite call.

Ballad of Miss Sally

Miss Sally lay on her cornshuck bed,
Old and alone and poor,
In her tumbled shack on the Buck Thorn hill,
With dirt for its kitchen floor.

Miss Sally lay on her cornshuck bed.
She was dying of gangrene;
For she'd broke her hip, and she'd crawled to bed,
And the neighbors had not seen.

The neighbors came, and they found her there,
And they called Relief in town;
Relief-man came to Miss Sally's house
And his money blank laid down.

"Sign your papers?" Miss Sally laughed,
"I've silver to do and more;
A hundred thousand my father left,
And it's hid in the kitchen floor."

The neighbors came, and they called Relief,
And after the things they said—
The health nurse came with her laundry sheets
To put on Miss Sally's bed.

"Keep your sheets for I have my own—
And all of the linen fair;
Forty sheets in my mother's press,
And it's locked in the corner there."

The neighbors came with their gifts of food.
"Plenty I keep myself,
Bread and honey and golden cream,
All hid on my cupboard shelf."

The doctor came to Miss Sally's house,
For he knew Relief would pay.
"Cures I mix in my old black pot,
And I'll walk at the dawn of day."

Ballad of the Rest Home

I saw four silver ponies
Come swimming in from sea,
And on the four, across the shore,
My loved ones came to me.

I leaned from out the window;
I called—they heard me call;
The nurses came and took me;
They stood me by the wall.

I saw the gray wall open;
I saw them all again;
I saw *five* silver ponies
Come rising from the main.

The fifth was newly bridled;
His feet were nailed with fire;
I took my match and lit it
And waited in the pyre.

My pony stood before me;
I mounted him and turned;
The others rode beside me,
And all the glory burned.

We rode the waves at sunset;
And so they took me home. . . .
At dark, five silver ponies
Went down into the foam.

West Virginia

Where the mountain river flows
And the rhododendron grows
Is the land of all the lands
That I touch with tender hands;

Loved and treasured, earth and star,
By my father's fathers far—
Deep-earth, black-earth, of-the-lime
From the ancient oceans' time.

Plow-land, fern-land, woodland shade,
Grave-land where my kin are laid,
West Virginia's hills to bless—
Leafy songs of wilderness;

Dear land, near land, here at home—
Where the rocks are honeycomb,
And the rhododendrons . . .
Where the mountain river runs.

Garden Moment

Forty years I lived,
Never saw before
What I saw this morning,
And if forty more—
Though I watch forever,
Straining patient eyes—
Shall I see such other
Miracle arise:
See the brown earth cracking—
Rupture of the night—
And the seed, the flower,
Rising to the light.

Coal Fern

The green ferns that lift from the forest's damp floor
Grow full in the autumn and scatter their spore;
The white ferns that silver the frost of the glass
At midnight will come and at morning will pass.

But the black fern that lies in the coal's hidden seams
Still treasures the quantum's primordial streams
From the sun of the lost suns that died long ago
When the dinosaur quaked on the edge of the snow,
And the great pterodactyl's reptilian flight
Sent down on the fern-trees the shadow of night.

Then the great silent fern-trees in darkness decayed
And treasured and measured and captured and laid
The core of the atom in infinite shade.

Ballad of New River

Ancient of rivers—called the New—
Oldest of all earth's streams—
Flowing here when *Tyrannous Rex*
Walked in his lizard times.

Glaciers melted, the silt walls washed,
Damming the westward run.
The river turned like a captured beast;
The Ohio gulped it down.

But east of the capture, the New was old,
River of earth and time,
Moving on through the shadowed wild,
Deep in its canyoned flume.

The bison came to the waterside,
And the wild swans floated still;
The Cherokee and the Shawnee brave
Passed by on the river trail.

The white men trekked by its rocky shores—
The lean, tall, hunter men—
The frail canoes on its current rode,
And the ox-bowed wagons ran.

The wagons crossed as they trundled west;
Then the soldiers, gray and blue,
Bled out their lives in the river's mist,
And the railroads tunneled through.

The boats of oil and the boats of coal
Slugged past on the river's weight;
The forests fell, and the logs swept down
When the elder bloom was white.

Sulphur water and tannery ooze,
And the black, raw sewage crawled;
The New moved on through its stinking maze,
Heavy and rank and coiled.

Lizards may go and lizards return,
And the hominids depart,
But the New flows on through the oak and fern
Of the forest's mended heart.

Ancient of rivers—called the New—
Oldest of all earth's streams—
Flowing now where *Tyrannous* stalks,
Raising his lizard combs.

🌳 *Gauley Mountain*

Arrow Grasses by Greenbrier River

Arrow grasses by the river,
Phalanx, spear by spear arrayed,
Teach us that we may remember
Others here have walked afraid.

Teach us—all our generation—
We are not the first to know
Death and war and red transgression
Where these quiet waters flow.

Long ago our father's father
Here in springtime dropped his corn,
Died and fell, an arrow winging
In his heart that April morn—

Dead as you and I will ever
Lie beneath the atom's burst—
Arrow grasses by the river,
Teach us we are not the first,

Nor the last to live in danger,
Live in wonder and in woe,
Here on earth beside the river,
Where the quiet waters flow.

Gabriel MacElmain, Pioneer

He climbs the eastern slope to stand
Upon the backbone of the range,
And there across that brutal land
A hundred seasons change.

He does not see the hulking shade
Where Delaware and Mingo pass,
But slopes where well-fleshed cattle wade
Knee-deep in bending grass.

Soft furrows rolling from his share
Run straight across that brushy plain,
And swinging boughs of peach and pear
Sow broadcast up his lane.

He watches long. His pack mare stamps
And flicks her tail. He watches still . . .
To see the squares of farmhouse lamps
Against that timbered hill.

His pack mare strains upon her rope
And turns to nuzzle at his face,
Then down the Gauley's western slope
He breaks a footpath for his race.

The Clearing

He set his claim upon the bark
Of corner oaks with lawless mark.
And while the April moon was low
To dry the sprouts which fought to grow,
He banded every tree with doom,
So sun might pry into the gloom
To pull the blades of life from grain.
He'd drop the corn across the plain
When dogwood blossoms curving round
Gave him the sign that mountain ground
Was warm enough to make seed swell
Breaking the hardened golden shell,
Thrusting the green spear which would make
The silk-wrapped ear to grind and bake
In dodger, pone, and johnnie cake.

The Flame

Where limestone water cleft a time-worn ledge
To spread its moving silver as a fan
And rim the bluegrass with a curve of foam,
He paced a five-yard square between the edge
Of jagged gulch and where the wild began
And drove four hickory stakes into the loam.

He rolled four gray, unpolished blocks
Unto the corners, tamped them there
And squinted till he got them plumb.
Of hand-hewn logs and hand-dressed rocks
He built his cabin strong to bear
The unleashed force of winds to come.

The evening when he hung the puncheon door
He tried the leather hinges, raised the latch,
And thankful of his labor near at end,
Passed through, scraped up dry shavings from the floor,
Struck flint against his knife and watched flame catch
Upon the rugged hearth his sons would tend.

Cornelius Verner

Fenced in by need his youth had passed,
So now greed spliced his chain and fast
He measured hills and quickly stepped
Till dark fell on him; then he slept
Uneasily until the dawn
When he could drive his conquest on.

At twilight of the seventh day
He closed the lines of one survey;
And wondered if he had his share
Distinctly marked so none would dare
Question his patent or transgress
Upon his plotted wilderness.

The plains of Holland stretched so wide
To sea-drawn curves on every side,
And he had journeyed west alone
With his intention set to own
Such stretches of infinity,
As need no dikes to check the sea.

But in this snare of hill-pressed gloom
He smothers from a lack of room.
The great new world deceives—but still
There's much of it a man can till;
And every mountain hides two more,
And every valley is a door.

And there are many trees to mark
With blazes deeper than their bark,
And many borders to define.
Now Irish thief and English peer
And Shawnee chief and spotted deer
Must stop before his trespass sign.

Katchie Verner's Harvest

It pleasures her to gather
A hoard when autumn comes:
Of grapes in scroll-worked silver,
Red-streaked-with-amber plums,
Winesaps and seek-no-farthers,
Green peppers, russet pears,
White roastin'-ears for drying
On frames above the stairs,
Queer handled gourds for dishes
And dippers at the spring,
Long butternuts, fat pumpkins,
Cream-colored beans to string,
Wild meats to jerk and pickle,
Brown chestnuts tipped with cold,
Cranberries from the marshes,
Tree honey dripping gold.

In barrels and crocks and suggins,
In pokes upon the floor
And hanging from the rafters
Is Katchie Verner's store
Against the mountain winter
When sleet-hard drifts will freeze
The deep loam of her garden
And gird her orchard trees.

Oil Field

A crawling black transgressor
Old Verner never feared
Has undermined the meadow
Which he surveyed and cleared.
A pipe of soldered metal
That runs with yellow oil
Glides down a hidden furrow
Beneath his fallow soil.
And round that lengthened skyline
The steel-ribbed derricks stand
Like windmill ghosts arisen
To haunt Old Verner's land.

Lydia Verner

What shall I do with the Verner money?
Finance a show?
Or trade it in with my youth's wild honey
For a gigolo?

How shall I cover the Verner body
Of a peasant frau?
With silk or velvet or cotton shoddy?
No one cares how.

How shall I surfeit the Verner craving
For land and more,
When the silver blade of the road is shaving
The grass at my door?

The Son

End of a road,
End of a quest,
And now I feel the earth's heart beat
Against my breast.

End of a calling road,
I cannot understand.
I only know I have come back
To plow my father's land.

Pioneer Lullaby

Hush-ah-hush, hush-ah-hush, lullaby,
Sure your father will home at the morn
With salt and a grinding of corn,
Hush-ah-hush, hush-ah-hush, do not cry
For the crack in the door isn't wide. . . .
Hush-ah-hush, hush-ah-hush, hours fly
Though the wolves gnaw the deer bones outside.
Hush-ah-hush, hush-ah-hush, see how high
Our pine knots are sending their light. . . .
My girleen must slumber tonight,
Hush-ah-hush, hush-ah-hush, lullaby.

(There's a thatch-sheltered cottage in the County of Clare
With a white sanded floor . . . it were best to be there,)

But the elf folk who dance by the far-flowing stream
Remember and watch so my girleen may dream
With her winkers closed fast and her head pillowed deep,
Ah hush ye, ah hush ye, ah hush ye to sleep. . . .
(Mother in Heaven, look down, hush her cry!)
Hush-ah-hush, hush-ah-hush, lullaby.

Granny Saunders

Her ministration was to heal
With pungent herb and bitter peel.
Up in the drying loft she hung
Horehound and sage and blacksnake-tongue,
Wild cherry, spicebush, "penny rorrel,"
Blue monkshood, ginseng, sour sorrel,
Thin twisted stalks, sharp jimsonweeds,
Bloody percoons, hot mustard seeds,
And meadow docks—both broad and narrow,
Rough boneset, golden thread, and yarrow,
Field balsam, catnip, dittany,
All to be simmered down to tea.

All to be brewed for aches and ills—
Red pepper pods for croup and chills;
Spearmint for phthisic; flax for pain;
Horseradish roots for bruise or sprain;
And for uncertain maladies
The northwest bark of dogwood trees.

And, 'pon my word, before the British came
I recollect a night, hant-cursed and wild,
When Joe McKeever came and got me out
To help his woman with her slow-born child.

I took the babe, blew breath into its mouth,
And tied its navel with a linen thread.
It lived an hour and just before it died
It raised up chipper as you please and said,
"A warm winter and a cold spring,
A bloody summer and a new king."

Martha MacElmain

Since Josh was in the Northwest woods with Clark
And Granny Saunders watched another bed,
She was alone with birth, then with her dead
Until an admonition from the dark
Strengthened her courage. Well, the ground was rough
And had been frozen hard since early fall,
This hemlock tree was closely branched and tall,
The hole between its roots was wide enough
But needed deepening. . . . Yes, a trough of bark,
Lined with the silk of Grandma Renick's shawl,
Dirt and some willow buds. . . . well, that was all:
Her man was in the Northwest woods with Clark,
When he came back they'd have the preacher sent.
She passed along the timber, crossed the sands
To Gauley River, dipped her swollen hands,
Dried them on wisps of blowing air and went
Along the footpath, up the jagged shore.

While passing by her woodpile roofed with snow,
She thought by now her hearth-fire guttered low,
And kneeling just outside the cabin door,
Gathered some bark strips edged with frozen clay
And bundled them into her apron sack.
Then quavering a psalm, went in the shack
To poke the embers up and wait for day.

Jane Renick MacElmain (1)

I loved the children. Yes, and I loved Tim,
It wasn't that I thought myself too good,
But through the many nights I waked by him
My blood ran slower than a woman's should.
And it was cold there in our lean-to shack,
Each winter brought another mouth to fill,
And in the summer houseflies left a track
Of dung across my whitewashed windowsill.
My only dress was dyed in walnut bark,
Wild briers reached to claw my pansy bed,
Then lye soap turned the Renick linens dark
And wood mice left their toothprints on my bread.

One Sunday afternoon I went alone
To pick some horehound for the baby's tea,
And felt a quaking fever at my bone
When Donald Elson came and blandished me.
We left that night. I could not tell them why.
They would have thought my reason wild and vain;
He called me "Sweet" and told me he would buy
Bright shawls and dresses and a ruby chain.

Her shroud was made of walnut drab,
Her white pine box was plain.
She lay stiff-necked, impenitent
Without her ruby chain.

They interceded with a prayer,
Then left her to be still
Where mountain shadows creep like hants
Across the frozen hill.

A ruby torque around my throat,
A bronze and scarlet sheath,
And perfumed folds of saffron earth
Above me and beneath.

A windless and a tideless hush
Along this amber sand,
A gold-fringed orchid spray to lie
Like velvet on my hand.

Donna MacElmain

The hills and the night and your love are last seclusion.
No world remains but this.
No memory of my somber-winged confusion
Invades your kiss.
The sinuous road of the age unwinds no longer
Its bright, elusive charms.
My will to go free was forever strong, but stronger
Your bronzed arms. . . .

Which now lie impassive and cold and undemanding,
Assuming that their mark
Of knowledge on my body is withstanding
The portent dark.

Beloved, awake unto your need for keeping
The only-once-possessed.
Oh, twice unfaithful! That you can lie sleeping
So near my breast!

Susan O'Kane

Her back is bent beneath a million loads
Of wood and berries, water, hill-dwarfed grain;
Her eyes are sunken in the darkness, lone,
Half-lidded, dumb with pain;
Her hands are stubs, twice frozen to the bone;
And like time's etching on a gray hill stone,
The naked lines reveal upon her face
The story of a god-forgotten race.

Nora O'Kane

She was O'Kane and O'Kanes were white trash
Who lived in a cabin up Pheasant Run.
They seasoned their fodder beans with groundhog,
Borrowed their bread stuff and stole for fun.

All the O'Kanes had an Old Nick temper.
Their feet sashayed to the fiddle's tune,
And they could go to a patch of ginseng
Like their hound dogs followed a corn-fed coon.

Zeb Sage was old when he married Nora
To brute and carry and do his will,
And the Sages called her a scheming hussy,
But she ruled the Sages and rules them still.

Her brown feet jigged to the hymns they quavered.
Her hot blood swept through their torpid veins.
She signed her *X* in the family Bible,
And filled their cradles with dark O'Kanes.

Tillie Sage (1)

A stranger lives in the Sages' mansion
And a fiddle hangs on the parlor wall.
A red colt runs in the Sages' pasture
And a hound dog sleeps in the Sages' hall.

O wind, blow cold from the north-blue autumn,
O wind, blow hot from the brazen south,
Sculpture the lines of my golden body. . . .
Press your strength to my rose-stained mouth!

Down in their brick and brownstone town house
My dull Sage cousins knit and sew
On pants and gowns for the naked heathen
They would convert to a creed of woe.

But I ride the hills on a colt unbroken,
Ride the hills on a colt unshod!
I will not reach for their precious money
Nor bend my head to their wrathful god.

I might have need for the swathes of virtue
If my legs were bowed and my face were plain. . . .
O wind, blow hot from the brazen southland
On the red-haired daughter of Nora O'Kane!

Tillie Sage (2)

I broke a thorn from a leaning crab tree
To pin the rags of my shoddy dress.
I ran through the woods but the branches molded
The moving form of my nakedness.

I slept in the grass of Sage's pasture,
But the sun waves flowed through an ice-blue arc,
And drowned my blood in a golden torrent
And bore my dreams through a tropic dark.

I tore a rose from a climbing brier
And touched my lips to its center dew,
When I searched my face in a pool of water
My face was stained with a blood-like hue.

I lay on the ferns by the pool and sifted
The spores of fern from the grains of sand,
But I felt the stir of a live thing moving,
An earth-pulse throbbing beneath my hand.

I moved, and the crushed fronds slowly lifted
In the hollow curves where my breasts had lain,
I braided up my hair and went forth seeking
My stint of glory—and my lot of pain.

Tillie Sage (3)

What shall I say to you all as you watch me dying?
Shall I moan of terror or shall I whine of shame,
Or ask forgiveness that this child I leave you
Must bear my own and not its father's name?

What shall I say to all you pious Sages,
Waiting the crumble of my tight-walled heart?
Waiting to hear the quiver of confession
Break through my teeth and force my lips apart?

What shall I say as you hover there at my bedfoot?
Shall I speak of mercy, or shall I speak of sin?
Bend near and look. My neck is stiff forever . . .
As it has ever been.

Jed Kane

The Gauley mail was overdue
When Jed who was to drive it through
Cheat Mountain Pass to Staunton Run
Got special word from Washington—
In which a postal clerk inquired
Why Mr. Kane who had been hired
To drive the course at posthaste rate
Was not in yet, though three months late.

And now on a high-glazed marble wall
In the postal building Jed Kane's scrawl
Hangs framed in silver: "Respected Sir,
You ask the reason and this be her—
If the gable end blowed out of hell
Straight into the drifts of a snow that fell
Last fall on the ram's horn point of Cheat
It would take till Easter for brimstone heat
To melt a horsepath. So I remain.
Your obdt. svt., Jedson Kane."

Sol Brady

He could squint his eye up a white pine trunk
And guess its height to the saw-mill foot.
He could sleep straight up, he could pray when drunk,
And brain a man with his calk-heeled boot.

The women blushed at his blackguard talk
But the men swore loud by the name of Sol.
They lowered their jaws from his five-foot reach,
They drove his teams and they ate his swill.

He could pop the eyes from a balking horse
And wipe his thumbs on its flying mane.
He could ride three logs down the river's course
And shoot the head from a dropping pin.

One day Sol passed by an empty shack
And saw the end of a panther's tail
Stuck halfway out of a rotten crack,
He grabbed a holt and the cat was still.
Then he reached inside with his other hand
And choked the beast till its lungs caved in.
Sol's razor strop was a saw-mill band
And grab spikes grew from his knotty chin.

The Turnpike

Beneath a hundred years of thaw and freeze
The footprints of the bison blend in clay,
And branches snapped to mark a red man's way
Grow firmly knotted on their separate trees.
The turnpike which the slate-walled mountains squeeze
Was touched last evening with the twilight gray,
But it is bluer than the hills today
And iron horseshoes break its winding ease.
For Yankee horsemen riding three abreast
Have galloped on the pike since up-of-sun
And vanished through the rugged southern pass.
Virginians who took the wild trace west
Follow it back to where their blood will run
Seeking reunion in Virginia grass.

Traveler and Old Sorrel

The quiet pastures where they graze
Are blue with asters and the haze
Of Indian summer's smoky blur,
And only feathered drummers stir
The oak trunks with a dull tattoo,
While one thin breeze goes trailing through
The fields where Traveler and young Sorrel
Kick at the shining clumps of laurel
With saucy heels, toss back their manes
And race along clean-bordered lanes.

One with a coat of iron gray,
One with a coat of bronze-cast bay,
Colts with a mountain pedigree,
Marked with a common destiny;
(Manassas Junction and Gaines's Mill,
Harper's Ferry and Chancellorsville),
And fate astride them—they cannot know. . . .
Back to the shadowed fields they go,
Seeing the sunlight glint and pass
Over the plumes of orchard grass,
Over the pastures where they graze
Deep in the asters, under the haze.

Burying Field

Dwarf pine and yellow moonshine grass
Thrive on this dry, rejected land.
Hawkweed and bitter sassafras
Root-clutch their living from its sand.
Black ground was fenced for men to till.
The dead of Gauley own this hill.

The River

Now they have bridged the canyon of the Gauley
And built a lock above the Swago shoal
To float the barges past the lazy shallow
With loads of river sand and mountain coal.

Along the shore where passing Mingo warriors
Built driftwood fires to parch Ohio maize
Cook ovens glare red-eyed upon the darkness
And belch their cinders at the fevered days.

But in the broken rushes of the inlet
Where herons rose with beaten-winged alarm
That autumn evening when an Irish rascal
Knelt by the stream to bathe his wounded arm,
. . . White herons sleep, their folded wings unstained
By all that blood the savage Gauley drained
From pale-faced men whose kindred now possess
The last dark current of the wilderness.

🌳 *The Horsemen*

Corner Tree

This is the place it starts—
Beyond the Allegheny, where the primordial river parts the hill.
Here, from this old stump, the lines visible and invisible go
    westward,
The survey lines of a continent—

The old surveyors squinted into the sun's eye in the evening,
The old land lookers with their chains and tripods
    measuring west in the long summers.
The old maps eaten on the edges by silverfish and fire.
But their lines still there among the hobble bushes,
Straight lines where the ferns wander,
Straight over the tangles of grape, of scarlet woodbine.

And this old stump by the river, the tree that *was*.
The tree that was the beginning.
The great oak, pole oak.
Corner tree of the west.
Point of points.
The leafy father.
And all the other corner trees out of his straight lineage,
The unseen plumb bobs hanging from his first branches,
The mark-stones planted from his hard seed.

For two hundred years he stood here holding it all steady
    with his great bole:
Holding the borders of states, the blocks of townships,
Straightening the black furrow,
Stretching the barbed wire fences across Nebraska—
The sun's eye always moving toward the sea.

Rock-rooted on the bank of this Virginia river,
Drawing the river into his veins,
Leafing in the green Aprils,
Shedding in the fall winds,
But never budging—
Squaring up the old law suits,
Straightening the streets of cities,
The paddock bars,
The golden windrows;
Hanging the harps of bridges.
And still clutched fast to his ledges,
Girded the steel rails,
Braced the gatepost,
Marked the cornerstone with a purple lilac,
And tamed with his long parallelograms the wild acres,
The wild-running stallions,

The wilder dream.

The Autumn Drives
(Early 1800s)

The bison first surveyed this track,
But now a wider road
Curls up and down the mountain's back
And bears a darker load.

For on it through these autumn days
The nameless creatures plod,
While close behind the drivers raise
The whiplash and the prod.

The driven coffle of the slaves
On splayed and blistered feet
Goes south to market to be sold
To make the sugar sweet.

The cattle spotted white and red,
A shoving, frightened mass,
Go south so humans can be fed
On flesh of mountain grass.

The hogs—all sixty thousand hogs—
In herds of dusty black
Hoof slowly on their pointed legs
And waddle down the track.

From dawn to dusk eight weary miles
Toward Richmond far away,
So they can grin with apple smiles
Upon a Christmas tray.

Above the road, the vultures float,
For weakling things must fall
And die and slicken with the bloat
And wait the buzzard's call.

The scarlet leaves are on the wind;
The summer grass is low;
The empty pastures far behind
Are waiting for the snow.

But on and on down these ravines
And up this wooded shore,
The slave men trek to New Orleans,
The sheep to Baltimore.

The Horsemen

Who are these horsemen here riding and roaming over our
    forest trails?
Why are they combing each little patch of pine here on the
    river?
See how the hemlocks shake—
Why do they quiver?

Who are these nice rich men out of the city?
Come to our cabin doors—sober with pity—

Offer us fifty cents—hills by the acre—
Leaning upon our fence—
"Leave her or take her."

See how their watch fobs swing golden and shining.
Handing the deed to us . . .
Now we are signing.

See how their blue serge suits fit on the shoulders;
See how their blue eyes shine down through our boulders;
See how their watch fobs swing dancing and merry . . .
    Buying the River Coal,
    Buying the Cherry,
    Buying the old Tug Fork,
    Buying the Sandy,
Giving our little kids red sugar-candy.

Who are these men who ride off with the lawyers?
Talking of Elder Tide, speaking of sawyers,
Asking for hill galoots handy with axes,
Taking delinquent land, cheap for the taxes,
Searching the courthouse names,
    Thumbing the pages—
    Thousands of empty claims—
    Dust of the ages.

See how their blue eyes move trying to follow
Something that's underground, black in the hollow?
See how their blue eyes lift slow as a measure
Scaling the popular trunks?
What is their pleasure?

All of our hills so steep—no good for sowing—
Lonesome and rocky-deep, even for mowing;
Nothing but ups and downs . . . levels so shallow,
Lying one hundred years worthless and fallow;
Hills that are black and sheer, covered with timber—
Nothing a man could clear now to November—
Hills that our fathers found—bitter and narrow—
Coal that the ages wound black in the marrow . . .

Who are these nice rich men riding and riding?
See how their blue eyes move carefully sliding
Over the black that grows out of the ridges—
Talking of railroad grades, tunnels and bridges—
Money to burn and jobs,
Jobs for all takers—
Who are these men who ride?

"Movers and shakers."

Timber Boom

The Gauley fox can scent the maddened rattler
And dodge the swift uncoiling of his sheath,
But now an unknown dread is whirring, whirring . . .
And green dust spurts before its jagged teeth.

The white pines quake against the Gauley sunrise
And shudder till they crash down Gauley hills,
The trout float belly-upward on the river
With sawdust raking blood around their gills.

Only the worthless clumps of laurel and scrub oak
Give hiding to the rabbit and the deer,
Pine siskins flutter from the coneless branches
And groundhogs burrow downwards from the Fear.

A Boom is rolling southward over Gauley
And in its wake the hills lie starkly skinned,
But it is not the pealing wrath of thunder. . . .
And it is not the iron-fingered wind.

It rumbles from the hammers which are building
Slum shanties under fog,
(*Fifty a thousand and grub stake free at the cookshack*
For a white pine log.)

Log Drive

Now when the flood of April
Snorts by the gullied plain,
Pine logs are foaming stallions
Unbroken to the rein.

Sol Brady's woodhicks gallop
Down Gauley to the mill,
They bow their legs and straddle
And set their hooks with skill.

They leap, a-swopping horses
To scare the folks on shore,
And sing a logger ballad
Above the water's roar.

Tonight in Brady's cookshack,
Baked beans and logger stew . . .
And later, in the bunkhouse,
A keg of mountain dew.

So spur your calk heels, Bullies,
And gallop through the foam. . . .
Gee-haw your kant hook bridles
And guide your stallions home.

Saturday Night
(1890–1910)

Saturday night and the Brady loggers
Fresh from the Gauley camp,
Swaggering down to Slaven's Pigear
With their calk-heeled tramp.
Cash in their jeans and their saw-bent fingers
Knuckled with steel to fight.
 . . . Nary a street that a decent woman
Dare walk tonight.

Saturday night and loggers riding
Out on their weekly bust,
Back from the pike, for they scatter humans
As soon as dust. . . .
Up and down by the Baptist church house
Mocking the Free-from-Sin!
Oh, turn your ears to the horn of judgment
The hicks are in!

First Train
(1895)

At every stile and hitching post
Uneasy horses champ and rare.
Hill folk from twenty mile around
Are crowded on the depot square.
The upper island is a-work
For there the oxen barbecue,
And there are stacks of bakery bread,
And kegs of foaming lager brew.

Now loafers by the water tank
Thumb-stretch their galluses and spit
Tobacco juice a half foot short
Of marks they squint upon to hit.
For through the tunnel mouth she comes
With bellowings of fire and steam,
She grinds the rails, she splits the wind
With filings from her iron scream!

So grab your younguns, clear the track!
Today old engine Number Nine
Pants into town and opens up
The running over Gauley line!
So while the grub comes easy, eat.
And drink while spigots flow with beer. . . .
To the biggety bugs of the N&W
Who sent regrets they can't be here.

The Spark

The log train bellowed through the dark.
Its engine sowed one flying spark.
Two dry leaves smoldered in the air.
And then three leaves took up the flare.
Four sticks upon the forest floor
Like tindered wings began to soar.
And then the wind—five zephyrs blew;
And six dead hemlocks bursting grew
To seven hillsides ripped with light;
Then fourteen mountains seared the night that into Hell's
   inferno turned . . .

Forty thousand acres burned.

Deserted Lumber Yard

No longer do the Brady loggers harry
The folk of Swago town.
Along the tracks on this deserted siding
The lumber piles rot down.

No longer do the hills of Gauley tremble.
The boom has gone its way.
And left Sol Brady's lumber stacks to darken
In open-tombed decay.

The skidders have unhooked their chains and grab points,
Hung up their harness lines.
No calk-heeled boots molest this quiet siding,
This boneyard of the pines.

Reforestation

Brown tents are staked upon the slopes of Gauley
And star-sown banners fly
Or hang like rags against the windless dawning
Of Gauley sky.

A cookhouse stands once more where Swago waters
Have left their pebbled track
And slum-born youth climb up the sides of Gauley
To grub and hack.

The groundhog digs another winding burrow,
For now the C.C.C.'s
Are timbering the saw-razed slopes of Gauley
With white pine trees.

Saturday Night
(1930s)

Saturday night on the streets of Swago
And the C.C.C.'s are here
Strolling down to Slaven's poolroom
For their weekly beer.
Nails all clipped and their zipper jackets
Fastened up to the chin. . . .
Oh girls come out in your Roebuck rayons
For the Army's in!

Saturday night and the C.C. truckers
Stepping upon the gas . . .
Out of the road if your life is precious
And let them pass.
Up and down by the commerce building
Taunting the bourgeoisie. . . .
No sleep tonight, for the Brush Hook Legions
Are on a spree.

Stoic
(Circa 1907)

You, with the lamp and pick, what is your labor
In that dark and fetid hole
Where the black damp seeps and the black rats gnaw the
    timbers?

Stranger, I dig for coal.

And what will you do with your load that the flatcars carry
From this upper-shaft of hell,
And dump by the tracks for the loader crew to shovel?

Stranger, they pay me well.

And what will you do with the fourteen greasy dollars
That the payroll bosses give
In exchange for your load when the six-day week is over?

Stranger, a man must live.

And how will you live when the rocks of a gutted mountain
Shatter your beam-held sky,
And the rescue digs, and your wife goes blind with waiting?

Stranger, a man must die.

The Company
(Coal Miner)

The Company owned the houses,
And The Company owned the store;
The Company paid the Sheriff off,
And fixed the Schoolhouse door.

The Company owned the Baldwin-Felts,
And opened up the bar;
And set the tipple on its stilts,
And lit the Christmas Star.

They owned the mountain and the mine,
The river and its fork;

They summered in the Byzantine
And wintered in New York.

Best House They Was Ever In
(Retired Coal Operator)

In these mountains there was coal,
And the World War looming—
Railroads just begun to roll—
Prices—they were booming.

Now with *coal,* it doesn't come
Running from a spigot.
Miners—and they need a home
While they work to dig it.

And this country—back awhile—
Barren as November:
Not a town for thirty mile.
Nothing here but timber.

Miners couldn't help *themselves*—
Even build a hovel.
All they furnished on the job—
Just their pick and shovel.

Built them each a Jenny Lind,
Had them painted yellow—
Best house they was ever in—
Cabins—up the hollow . . .

Then a store so they could eat.
Then their kids, a teacher.
Built their church and graded school.
Even hired the preacher.

Now, I know the things they tell,
Grudges some still harbor—
Had to do it. Did it. Well?
Even got the barber.

With the shoestring that we had—
God, we had to hump it . . .
Call it *good* or call it *bad*—
Like it or you lump it.

Monongah
(December 6, 1907, Marion County, West Virginia, on the Monongahela River)

Tell in the wind of the singing of sorrow;
Read on this whiteleaf the dirge of the poor;
Stand on the bank of this north-flowing river;
Mark with your silence a cross on its shore.

Say that these men were from far-distant countries:
"Hunkies" and "Tallies," and Russian and Pole,
Welshman and Irish—then some from the mountains—
And all of them diggers, who dug in the coal.

See how they come to the portals that morning,
Lamps on their foreheads and lunch pails that shine;
See how they stand for a hesitant moment;
Watch how they vanish down into the mine.

Hear the first blast—how it shudders the mountains—
Now hear the others—the feedings of hell—
Then, like an answer, the cries of the women—
And all in a second—how utter it fell.

The four that got out . . . say they died in the morning,
Or else when the midnight had crawled on the shore;
And the gravediggers dug in the earth of the frost runes;
And each of the shanties—a wreath on the door.

Then say that they came where the torch seemed to beckon,
That torch by the ocean as bright as the sun—
Count on the stars over ill-starred Monongah;
Reckon the death toll:

Three-sixty-one.

Overheard on a Bus
(Miner's Wife)

He must go down in the mine—
It's all he knows;
Certain as morning shine
Then off he goes—
Me standing there in the door
A-seeing black
And wondering evermore
If he'll come back. . . .

Asked him, I have, to quit.
I can beg and whine,
But there's nothing to do for it,
It's the mine, the mine—
And him cast under its spell,
So off he goes—
Black as the mouth of hell,
And when it blows—
But I reckon they pay him well,
And it's all he knows. . . .

Winter Day
(Coal Country)

The slag pile seeps into the sulphured stream,
And tipple skeletons obstruct the day.
A strip mine high-wall, rearing, bleeds above
The broken shanties, and the children play
Along the sewer where the winter trees
Are black as mine-props holding up the storm.

The Hard Road

When the roads first came,
When they looped and curled through the rocky cuts,
When the cars first whirled,
When the roads first came with their silver gray,
When the houses far in the hills away
Came down to sit in their huddled rows
Along the edge where the silver flows—

When the schoolhouse leaned and began to move,
When the church came in from its maple grove,
When the barns moved down with their lean-to sheds
And all stood close where the silver threads—

When the silver threads with its strands of gray
When the young folks smiled,
When they went away,
When the plow horse died in the tractor's row,
And the ballad changed to a radio—

When the roads first came,
When they looped and curled through the rocky cuts,
When they brought the world,
When they leaped the gorge,
When they lowered the hill,
When they brought the world with its good and ill—

The Roads

Where do the roads go—
The ruined country roads flow,
Fern-clogged and weed-bogged, wandering the hills?
Nowhere that I know—by shad-blow and fencerow,
By woods where the lilacs grow,
By the rotted sills.

What can a road feel?
How can this sorrow heal?
Sole mark and wagon wheel passing through the day,
Grain load and apple load creaking down the hilly road—
All of the life that flowed—
Now gone away.

Where do the roads wind?
What do they go to find?
Crossing on the mountaintops and meeting by the shores,
Swamp-locked and briar-blocked, searching for the rib-
    rocked
Men of the mountain stock,
By their empty doors—

Frost-pocked and burr-docked.
Winding through the passes
Where the dying chestnut trees reach their shriveled arms—
Thorn-crossed and time-lost, through the tangled grasses—
All the little country roads,
Searching for the farms. . . .

The Great Depression

Who are these men tramping the roads
Day after day, packing their loads,
Looking for jobs, asking for chores?
Who are these men knocking on doors?

Who are these men standing in queues,
Waiting for soup, asking for news?

Who are these men sunburnt and worn
Out in the field, burning their corn?

Who are these men dumping our food
Into the sea—all of it good?

Who is this child, starving and pale?
What is the twist? Where did we fail?

Who are these men walking forlorn?
Who are these men burning their corn?
Who are these men dumping the wheat?
Who is this child—nothing to eat?
Who are these men hunting for jobs?
When will they turn, turning to mobs?
How is this land?

Rich as the plain,
Warm in the sun, sweet with the rain.

What is the twist?
Why is the pain?

Depression Wind
(Winter 1930)

Crawls through the yard fence,
Enters from the back,
Moans on the roof,
And runnels down the stack
Crying the message that all poor men know:

"Prices arc high, and wages are low,
And the baby sick with the quinsy-o."

Pasture Line Fence

Worry at night how I can fence the pasture—
Three mile at least—all up side-hill and down—
And wire so high—I looked in Sears and Roebuck
And asked them at the hardware up in town.
When work and rails was cheap, our grandad fenced it;
But that was eighty—nearly—years ago—
A good rail fence, but long since sagged and rotted—
I just don't know.

My father, though he tried, could never make it,
With all the price of fence wire gone so high—
Our chestnut dead for posts, so he would stake it
And patch it up with thorn brush—getting by—
And now *my* turn. I patch—the cattle wander
Over on Charlie Hinkle's. He's the same
And got no fences—all our mountain pastures
All run together cross-wise. It's a shame.
But still I think at night, and think, still keeping
How I can put a fence up—good and high—
As though old men could make it better sleeping
Out there upon the gravehill where they lie.

Threnody for Old Orchards

There is such sorrow here in these old orchards
That had I, of the Greek, some darker strain,
These *stadia* of hills should curve to answer,
And I would rant the echo of my pain.

Here was the fruited tree-land of my fathers,
And here the bended bough-land of the fall,
And here the winesap bending and the pippin,
And here the heartwood growing—and the gall. . . .

Gone is that time and gone my orchard country,
And all the fields and farmsteads of this plain;
And all so lost—so lost—the hardhack tangles,
And nettles choke the footpath and the lane—

And all so lost—and all so lost forever—
That had I, of the Greek, some tragic song,
Here, from the sounding well of this old orchard,
I would inflict my wrong
On all the world, and all the world would answer,
And draped in hairy garments, walk the stage,
And cry the death of kinsmen and of orchards,
And rage and rage and rage.

The Grave Creek Inscribed Stone

The stone tablet they found in the mound at Grave Creek,
With hieroglyphics or mystic runes carved there on its face
   as the copy shows it,
But the stone itself long stolen away—
Or broken—lost—
What words did it say?
Query the query forever.

Of a noble Adena king,
Of his wars, his conquest?

Or of sky-gods riding on white wings out of the west?
Or did it tell how to plant pumpkins, squashes, sunflower?

Or of that strange death-pox that swept the village,
Fever and black buboes and rotting bone?
Then, at the last, this one slow-dying scholar
Carving his terror inward on the stone.

Or of how copper is melted, where the copper veins run in
   the rock face beside the Lake of Winds?

Or did some old seer, mask-faced and gray, medicine man
   of all strong medicine, carve in fading eye-light
His one last message to the Earth?

Make no war among you.
Brother to brother speak before the long silence swells your tongue.
Offer work and seed to the One Only.
Drink not from the gourd of your in-laws.
Touch not your footsoles to the moon.
Joy in your hour of sunlight.
Beware the atom when it comes.

The Runaway Team
(Written a Few Days After John Glenn's Space Flight)

Forty-some years—and so far away,
But the journey set in my heartbeat still—
Dad and I with Old Bird and Bay
Drove a-milling to Holley's Mill,

With a sack of corn and a sack of wheat
Loaded in at the granary door;
Then the click of lines and the plod of feet,
And we swung adrift from our narrow shore,

Our wood-shod sled like a galley forth
At morning there on the snowdrift tide—
Barn behind us to clock the north,
And all before us the world, and wide

Snow-sea meadows and spinning spray
And crested waves on the ocean hill—
And Dad and I, with Old Bird and Bay,
Off a-milling to Holley's Mill.

Nine or ten in my new red coat,
With my leggings hooked and my ribbons prim,
And a bright new dime for a candy poke
At Holley's Mill on the farthest rim
Of earth, of space—for I dreamed it so
As we swung along in our sea-borne track
On the crest of time, with the miles to go—
All seven miles to the mill and back.

Forty-some years ago—Today:
The thrust to orbit, the blast-off count.
I touched the dial—a word to pray—
The camera turning—I watched him mount—

Yet I, the rider; his torque of space
My twisted circuit to loop and turn—
The fire storm blowing across my face;
Three sunsets flowing behind me burn.

Through bands of ether—through flaming hail—
Across the serpent—his tongue licks forth,
Its plasma glowing—the cosmic snail,
In splendor hanging, invades the North.

Beyond the splendor, across the sphere
Of lunar silence and polar deeps,
My orbit swinging—the one I fear
Is now the spider. The spider sleeps.
He is the spider. He is the sun.
Our kindly neighbor—his web is spun,
Magnetic meadows—his fiber flows
From out his belly—his belly grows
The more distended—the spider knows
But keeps his secret—Arachnid dreams
Await our coming—his strands devise
The mystic circuits, the solar streams;
Two hoods of amber obscure his eyes.
On his bed of neutrons our neighbor lies.

But I am passing his thralls of lace—
By shores of plasma, by flaming kill,
My capsule whirling the gulf, I trace
The thermal river, the quantum hill—
I was only going—the spider still,
Bemused and waiting—to Holley's Mill.
I was only going—his threads are spun—
To mill at Holley's—the golden one—

And I started out from a granary door
At dawn, with Dad, in our wooden sleigh—
And I still remember the coat I wore—
But something happened along the way—
Something frightened Old Bird and Bay.

Time Is Our House

I was marooned upon the island,
And so to pass the time away
I cut around this branch of alder
And marked each circle of the day.

For long I searched that strange horizon
But turned unto myself again.
I broke the withe and in its hollow
The present and the past were plain.

Time Is Our House

Time Is Our House

What race is mine, unnatural to earth,
That did not come and does not think to go,
That sees the sun eternally at noon,
But not the rising nor the falling low?
How stands our oak beneath the roof of glass,
Forever hanging cant-wise in the air,
Rootless, without a lineage in the rock,
And barren of the seed its kindred bear?
Time is our house, but at the east no door,
And from the west no pathway to the spring.
Even the track of winter on the shore
Has more than we to borrow and to bring.
Even the mother fox has more to say
Of what the winds may tide and blow away.

Cassandra

I sat by the window and trod my loom,
And I saw the shape of a gaunt mushroom
Grow up the iceberg and spread the sky;
And I wove in my cloth that the world would die.

The New Corbies

If trees remain and carrion crows
Still gather on the oak,
That morning when the green wind blows
And carries off the smoke,
The crows will find below them there,
All blooming from the ground,
As flowered and as fat a feast
As crows have ever found.

Of scarlet red and bloated white,
And flowered full in bloom
Those tropic blossoms all will burst
To waft their sweet perfume.

And floating from the oak tree's limb,
Like hunger, then the crows
Will taste of man and savor him—
The richest fruit that grows,
When from the forehead of his dream
Exudes the atom rose.

Then night will come, though not the "sable" night,
Though not the dark, the "wished for balm," the still. . . .
But deathly brightness, thermo-neutron night,
Until some star-mad watcher on a hill,
Across the galaxies will peer and cry
That where there once was nothing in the sky,
Now there is flame beyond the southward horn—
A small, new planet, risen fully born
In one wild surge of green and glowing birth,
And looking at it, he will name it
                                          Earth.

Potherbs
(Of the Edible Wild Plants My Granny Taught Me)

With fire to the eastward and fire to the west,
Then I may go hunting, with hunger possessed,
To break the harsh nettle, the blade of the sedge,
The fern and the toadflax, the flag on the edge
Of gullies, the crowfoot, the wild heron's bill;
I will hunt for the pokeweed upon that burnt hill—
Burnt hill of the atom, hot dust of the cloud—
If goose grass is living, I will not be proud.

Of Fitness to Survive

If the firefly and the glowworm
By their burning are in tune
With the structure of the atom
And are rendered thus immune,
In that light which follows darkness
But on which no darkness falls,
Then the *two* will feast and flourish,
Creeping down the embered halls—
Eating of the fire-egg burning
In the fire-hawk's flaming nest;
Sucking of the fire-milk flowing—
Lava from the fire-hag's breast.

Life-force

Alone on the rubble of Earth—all alone—
Alive in my body, and blood on the stone—
The black amanita, the hydrogen pall
Above me—I waken, and now I will crawl
For woundwort to heal me,
For leaf and for shoot
To feed me; with water
I suck from the root
Of arum; with shelter
I claw from the dust;
And with life from the welter
To draw as I must;
I will wrap me in bindweed
And comb out my hair
With thorn from the thornbush,
And southward repair
Across the burnt meadows,
And take to the wild—
Oh, sheath of the man-root
Beget me with child.

The Cave

In the caverns, where the light
Never filters through the night,
There the strange, albino things
Breed forever: bats with wings,
Leaf-veined fibers, thin as pearl,
And the blind worm's silver curl.

In the cave's unmottled dark,
There the white eel loops his arc,
There the blinded spiders spin,
Weaving, eyeless, out and in,
Catching frail, lactescent strands
In their whited spider hands.

Where the rivers of the mind
Subterranean must wind,
There the cobra rimed with snow,
Hooded, in the dark must flow;
And the wan iguana crawls
Plated lily, down the walls.

"Light"

Photon or wave, bullet or billow riding?
One second seven-split around the earth;
Dual dilemma, paradox abiding, hiding the heart
Of flame-heart in the flame—

Here at this burning crux the mystics stood,
While on them through the ages, showers fell,
Full golden showers streaming always down and never
   upward:
Nimbus, halo, sun, the aura, aureole, glory, glance, and fire,
Resplendence and effulgence, radiance, gleam,
Splendor, illumination, and the stream, ineffable, of beauty
From the One, Godhead or Brahma, Sun God, or the Son
   of man uplifted—

Principles, models, properties, and forms;
Formulas, graphs, refractions, and the lens;
But never yet the *Nature of* defined;
The thing itself more primal than the things
In terms of which description might be tried.

When the Scientists Told Me of the Expanding Universe

Farther and farther and far apart
As the universe expands,
How can I, reaching, still hold your heart?
How can I touch your hands?

Higher and higher the suns ascend
And lower the moons decline—
How can I keep to the burning end
Love of this love of mine?

How shall I hold as the cosmos spreads,
Keep as the worlds inflate—
How in the dust that the quasar sheds—
How shall I keep my hate?

To the Boys in Freshman History
(Thermopylae, 480 B.C.)

What can I tell you of the past
To guard you from the atom's blast
Unless the story of that day
The Spartans stood to bar the way?

Two hundred thousand Persians flowed,
A plumed river, up the road,
Three hundred Spartans, shield to shield,
To guard the passage—not to yield—
And yielded only one-by-one.
Old Sparta's children, son by son,
Struck upward, and the Persian fell;
For dearly bought what Spartans sell
The harsh old Mother teaches well.

And now, forever, Greece is free,
And on the plains of Thessaly
The sheep crop softly in the grass,
The road winds upward through the pass,
The dust of Persia silts the sea,
The shepherd guards Thermopylae.

The Turk and Nazi both are gone,
From Thrace the eagle of the dawn
Wheels southward—and the silver gulls
Of Skyros bank above the hulls
Of Xerxes' drowned argosy,
A salted trestle in the sea—
And still, forever, Greece is free.

And so what better can I say,
But tell you softly of that day
The Spartans stood to bar the way?
For them the arrow's flaming hiss;
For you the atom's gentle kiss;
But I must tell you—*tell* you this.

The Hounds

Terrors that bayed upon my track
And were eluded long ago,
Hungers of mind and heart come back
And trail your quarry through the snow.

This house is sleep, come drive me forth
That for an hour I may regain
The wild, swift wonder of my flight,
The living token of my pain—

That for an hour, I may be—
Hearing again your monster tongue—
The wild, fleet-footed thing I was,
The runner on the hills, the young.

Epitaph in the Imperative Mode

Let the clods fall, then silence and cold dew;
The sighing hush of snow, dark waters seep—
And all blue-shadowed twilights yet to come
Fall here and cover deep.

Autumns of drifting leaves,
Layer on layer whirl and blow;
Wind drift and earth's erosion bring
Foot upon foot of heavy deepness here,
Heavy enough to cover this frail thing

That, decently buried, now indecently
Knocks on the lid and all night long, all day
Cries out alive, oh, cover deep to drown—
Bury the sound—the all-too-human sound—
Wrap deep around in sodden leaves and clay
The little cry
That, of all others, frights the very world—
Frightens the world because it will not die.

Oh, quick grab from the north, the south—
Leaves, dirt, stone—stuff in the mouth—
Rocks on the throat to strangle out the scream
Of the unwelcome and undying dream.

The Passage of Time

Kill the bright cobra
Whose hood is the terror
Of loneness and darkness
And death in the mirror;

Kill the gold python
Who hangs in the forest—
Whose way is by winding
By dearest and nearest;

But fear the clear serpent
Transparent as morning
Who glides without color—
So soft is his turning

He flows on the grass,
And the grass is not flowing—
He breathes on the leaf,
And the leaf is not blowing.

The Verb

This is the crystal verb,
The ultimate tetrahedron,
After all else is gone.

This is the primal core
In the boulder's marrow.
Seek, you will find it there
Clear beyond sorrow.

Elegant, cold and white
With its facets shining—
Neither the *should* nor *might*
Nor the *may* nor *can be*—

Only the crystal form alone and silent,
Pure to its inmost depth, its axes running.
Gemstone of years—the angled *krystallos* prism.

Take it then in your hand—
Icy and hard,
The flawless symmetry
That *Is* is *Is*—
Hard-cut.
Cold.
And clear.
And elegant.

Wife

I will not go with you where dark spears scatter
The red magnolia bough,
Nor to the April meadows where your furrow
Rolls clean beneath the plow.
I will not follow where the hearth fire gathers
Your kinsmen and my foe.
To the bright hill where all men seek the battle
I may not go.
I will not walk again in shoes of silver
The pathway none prolongs.
I will not hear again, my own throat aching,
Love's brief, first songs.

But on the way we would not ease nor shorten,
By fallow lands our springs cannot renew,
Past the well and the rock and the stump, to the earth and
    morning,
I will go with you.

Backward Flight

Tell me again the birds are flying southward,
Tell me again they leave the woods and go,
Crying the lone cry from the weary sunset—
Bright wings before the snow.

Tell me again, but I will not believe you,
For every autumn when the haw trees burn,
Across this hilltop of the dying ember
I see the birds return.

The robin and the redwing and the sparrow,
The meadow lark and wren.
Out of my youth, that land of South and summer,
They come to me again.

Over the Mountain

When I was a child and we lived at home
In our farmhouse under the mountain's comb,
The meadows stretched from our wide front door,
And the fields ran down to the river's shore;
But behind our house, to the west and north,
The mountain reared, from the earth reared forth—
A king of dark, with a rocky crown,
The mountain stood, and its dark fell down
In shadowed length on our wide front door,
Across our fields to the south and shore.

When I was a child and we lived and grew,
My four tall brothers had work to do
And hills to run when their work was through;
But I, the dreamer, and of them all
The only sister, so lone and small,
Was always different since I was born,
My one leg twisted like gnarly thorn—
Four tall brothers, but I the lorn
Child who sat by the backyard tree
And staring, staring, could almost see
Across the mountain and over far,
North and westward by wind and star.

"Over Bonnie"—the tales they told—
When I was little the words were gold;
"Bonnie River" and "Over Yon,"
"Across the Mountain" and on and on
Where I had never, *have* never gone.

My four tall brothers and Gramp and Pa
Ran the ridges and rooked the law,
And every June time and every fall,
At brook trout rising and turkey call,
Crossed the mountain. I watched them fade
Up morning ridges, through tear-mist shade
Until they vanished; yet leaf-tread still
I walked behind them down Galford hill,
Across the hacking, through rocky gate;
The pine wind touched me—my leg was straight.

A week. I waited. One sunset burned;
Then six tall hunters that night returned,
Dropping downward through files of gloom,
With trout and turkey and wild bee comb—
"Mama, Mama! It's them, come home!"

*   *   *   *

When I was a child—as I am no more,
For I left my place by our back yard door,
And east and south were the fields stretched wide,
South and east by the river's side,
Where the long, green meadows, swinging glide—
I found my city, my brace, my pride.
Found this city . . . so bright and bare,
But still at evening on street and stair,
When stars moved over, I always yearned
North and westward. When starlight burned
Above the smokestacks, I turned my eyes—
King and Monster, I saw it rise
Above my city, my safe-lit town—
That hill of granite, that rocky crown.

On penthouse roof and at the subway gate,
I turned, and turn, and always, soon or late,
As now, this evening still . . . for visions do fulfill,
Arising not at will, but of themselves, by power yet
    unknown . . .
And I have walked, a thousand nights, that hill,
Beneath my feet each loved, familiar stone,
And known, by heart, the pathways where they wind,
So well that I could walk them with the blind,
And find, and surely find . . .

    I know that country . . . every brake of laurel, the long
Savannahs, scent of pennyroyal, the pine wind blowing—
Waters gray and wild
And always farther, farther—dream-beguiled—
Across to Bonnie River—undefiled.

In some strange room when ether brings the night
In waves descending downward on my sight,
Then will I track my hunters—gone before—
And all lean, lawless hunters of that shore—
Beyond the mountain, through the rocky crown,
Across the green savannahs flowing down
In tides of bluegrass westward where they roll—
Forever, farther, farther—"Bonnie Shoal."

Author's Notes
Bibliography

"American Boating Song (1939)"   This poem was first published in *Time Is Our House*. It was reprinted in *Paradox Hill* with the title "Boating Song."

"Wire Brier"   The title comes from a children's counting rhyme: "Wire brier, limber lock, / Three geese in a flock. / One flew east and one flew west, / One flew over the cuckoo's nest."

"Ballad of New River"   The prehistoric New River—called by geologists, the "Teays"—once ran north and west from North Carolina into Illinois, where it received the tributary waters of the ancient Mississippi and then flowed south to an embayment of the Gulf of Mexico. When the glaciers melted, the river was dammed behind silt walls and "captured" by the Ohio. Although it is doubtful that any of the earth's rivers can accurately be called "the oldest," the New River, east of Nitro, West Virginia, still flows in its primordial channel, as it has for several million years.

"Gauley Mountain"   The poems in this section are largely taken from the verse narrative of a fictional land called "Gauley." Names, characters, places, and incidents are imaginative amalgamations; any resemblance to actual persons (living or dead), or events, or locales is entirely coincidental.

"The Son"   This poem was first published in *Mountain White*. A slightly different version appeared in *Gauley Mountain* with the title "Helmit Verner—1918."

"Jed Kane"   The letter on which this poem is based really existed and was, for many years, in the U.S. Postal Service offices in Washington, D.C. It was written by a man named Trotter who carried the mail. I changed the name of the mail carrier to "Jed Kane" and put the contents of the letter into verse.

"Traveler and Old Sorrel"   Traveler and Old Sorrel were the horses of General Robert E. Lee and Stonewall Jackson. I have no proof that these horses shared the same pedigree or that they ran together as colts, although they may have. They did participate in the Civil War battles named in the second stanza of the poem.

Author's Notes

"Corner Tree"   A corner tree is used by surveyors as a marking point.
The first recorded corner tree on the western waters was marked by
John Lewis on the Greenbrier River in 1751. Whether the Lewis Oak
or some other great tree was the "pole oak," the poetic metaphor
stands.

"The Autumn Drives"   Before the coming of the railroads, many
western Virginia farmers drove their livestock to market on the hoof.
One old record states that, in the fall of 1826, sixty thousand hogs
traveled along the James River and the Kanawha Turnpike, hoofing it
toward Richmond at the rate of eight miles a day. In the years before
the Civil War, Virginia sold its surplus slaves to "the cotton and the
cane," and a slave coffle was also a common sight on the turnpike.

"The Horsemen"   In the period from about 1850 to 1915, and particu-
larly from 1865 to 1900, many riders passed along the mountain trails.
These "horsemen" were timber buyers, mining engineers, and other
"land lookers."

"Timber Boom"   This is one of several poems I have written about
the timber boom which began about 1880 when the white pine loggers
first came to West Virginia and began to river-drive the logs. Later
the railroads came to take the hardwoods which were too heavy to
float out. This poem was first published in *Gauley Mountain*. I have
also written a prose account of the timber boom in *The Milkweed
Ladies* (Pittsburgh, Pa.: University of Pittsburgh Press, 1988). The
timber industry is still alive in West Virginia, but the fifteen million
acres of virgin forest are gone.

"The Spark"   The logging railroads were notorious incendiaries, and
the slashings left in the wake of the loggers were tinder-dry. Typical
of the forest fire problem was the Great Fire of 1908 that burned
1,703,850 acres of West Virginia forest.

"The Company"   The "Baldwin-Felts" were private detectives in the
hire of the mine operators.

"Best House They Was Ever In"   The typical coal camp house was
called a "Jenny Lind."

134

Author's Notes

"Monongah"   This poem is based on an actual mine disaster in Marion County, West Virginia, December 6, 1907. The estimate of the dead in this disaster totaled more than 361 since there were many "unlisted" boys working down in the mines with their fathers. Other West Virginia mine disasters—to list only a few—include: Eccles, 1914 (81 killed); Layland, 1915 (112 killed); Benwood, 1924 (199 killed); Bartley, 1940 (91 killed); and Farmington, 1968 (78 killed).

"Winter Day (Coal Country)"   A version of this poem was published in *Elderberry Flood* as one stanza of "Outlines in Black and White."

"The Grave Creek Inscribed Stone"   In 1838 the largest of West Virginia's Adena Mounds, the Mammoth Mound near Moundsville, was opened. Among the various relics found was, presumably, a small stone inscribed with strange hieroglyphics. A copy of this writing was made, but the stone itself subsequently disappeared and has been somewhat discredited. There is, however, no proof that the stone was a hoax. The poem is a speculation on what it might have said.

"Time Is Our House"   This poem was first published in *Time Is Our House* and then reprinted in *Paradox Hill* with the title "They—The Provincials of Time."

Bibliography

Note: This bibliography first lists alphabetically the books of poetry published by Louise McNeill. Following each title is an alphabetical list of the poems from each book that were selected for inclusion in this collection. New poems, and those reprinted from magazines, are listed separately at the end.

Elderberry Flood: The History, Lore, and Land of West Virginia Written in Verse Form. Charleston: West Virginia Department of Culture and History, Elderberry Books, 1979.
"The Autumn Drives (Early 1800s)"
"Best House They Was Ever In (Retired Coal Operator)"
"Coal Fern"
"The Company (Coal Miner)"
"Corner Tree"
"Depression Wind (Winter 1930)"
"Fiddler (1976)"
"First Train (1895)"
"The Grave Creek Inscribed Stone"
"The Great Depression"
"The Hard Road"
"The Horsemen"
"Monongah (December 6, 1907, Marion County, West Virginia, on the Monongahela River)"
"The Spark"
"West Virginia"

Gauley Mountain. New York: Harcourt Brace, 1939; rpt. Parsons, W. V.: McClain Printing Company, 1960, 1990.
"Burying Field"
"The Clearing"
"Cornelius Verner"
"Deserted Lumber Yard"
"Donna MacElmain"
"Faldang"
"The Flame"
"Gabriel MacElmain, Pioneer"
"Granny Saunders"
"Granny's Story"

"Jane Renick MacElmain (1)"
"Jane Renick MacElmain (2)"
"Jed Kane"
"Katchie Verner's Harvest"
"Log Drive"
"Lydia Verner"
"Martha MacElmain"
"Moonshiner"
"Mountain Corn Song"
"Nora O'Kane"
"Oil Field"
"Pioneer Lullaby"
"Reforestation"
"The River"
"Saturday Night (1890–1910)"
"Saturday Night (1930s)"
"Sol Brady"
"Susan O'Kane"
"Tillie Sage (1)"
"Tillie Sage (2)"
"Tillie Sage (3)"
"Timber Boom"
"Traveler and Old Sorrel"
"The Turnpike"

Mountain White. Dallas, Texas: Kaleidoscope Press, 1931.
"The Son"

Paradox Hill: From Appalachia to Lunar Shore. Morgantown: West Virginia University Libraries, 1972.
"After the Blast"
"Arrow Grasses by Greenbrier River"
"Ballad of Joe Bittner"
"Ballad of Miss Sally"
"Ballad of New River"
"Ballad of the Rest Home"
"Blizzard"
"Cassandra"

Bibliography

"The Cave"
"Chestnut Orchard"
"The Dream"
"First Flight"
"Fox and Geese"
"Garden Moment"
"Hill Song"
"How to Unbewitch a Backtracking Hound"
"Involved (The Spider)"
"Life-force"
"'Light'"
"Lost in Orbit"
"Mayapple Hill"
"Memoria"
"The New Corbies"
"Of Fitness to Survive"
"Overheard on a Bus (Miner's Wife)"
"Overheard on a Bus (Woman with a Cleft Palate)"
"Over the Mountain"
"The Passage of Time"
"Pasture Line Fence"
"Poet"
"Potherbs (Of the Edible Wild Plants My Granny Taught Me)"
"The Roads"
"The Runaway Team (Written a Few Days After John Glenn's
     Space Flight)"
"Stories at Evening (A Suburban Mother Tells Stories to Her Son)"
"To the Boys in Freshman History (Thermopylae, 480 B.C.)"
"When the Scientists Told Me of the Expanding Universe"
"Wire Brier"

Time Is Our House. Middlebury, Vt.: Middlebury College Press, 1942.
     "American Boating Song (1939)"
     "Aubade to Fear (Heavy with Child)"
     "Hill Daughter"
     "Second Sight (My Son's First Springtime)"
     "Snow Angels"
     "Threnody for Old Orchards"

Bibliography

"Time Is Our House"
"Warning"

"Backward Flight" first appeared in *The Christian Science Monitor*.
"The Hounds" first appeared in *The Oregonian* (Portland). Poems
published here for the first time are "Epitaph in the Imperative
Mode," "Lullaby," "Stoic (Circa 1907)," "The Verb," "Wife," and
"Winter Day (Coal Country)."